Apple Garnishing

From:
International Culinary Consultants

Harvey Rosen

Kevin O'Malley

With full-color photos and step-by-step instructions

Recognition

Acknowledgements

Dedication:

To My Family...."The Apple of My Eye"...
Ann, Vicky, Debbie, Larry, Bob, Jon

Acknowledgement For Contributions and Assistance is Gratefully Made To:

Chef Kevin O'Malley, GM
Instructor of garde manger at
Hudson County Community College.

The author is indebted to the **International Apple Institute**, McLean, Va. for editorial assistance, materials and photographs in the development and publication of *Apple Garnishing.*

Fred Corey:
The Apple Industry is better today because of his ability and perseverance in effectively spreading the good word about apples.

Keffier V. Adkins
Art Director/Artist

Vince Serbin
Photographs

Published by:
International Culinary Consultants
P.O. Box 2202 Elberon Station
Elberon, New Jersey 07740

ISBN 0-9612572-7X
Printed in U.S.A.

From The Author

a Message

You are now ready to enter a culinary adventure. Use this book as a tool to explore the world of creative garnishing. Enjoy yourself as I enjoyed the process of probing the unlimited dimension of the apple.

Use this text as a guide. I have included easy to follow step-by-step instructions, diagrams, photographs and outlines to assure you success. Remember, above all, have fun and enjoy yourself not only in creating but in presenting your apple garnishes.

Chef Harvey Rosen, GM

Contents

Keeping The Apple Flesh White .. Page 26

Legends 5
Johnny Appleseed 6
Health and Nutrition. 7
Growing Apples, Hospitality, Favorite Pie 8
Juice and Cider 9
Buying, Handling, Storage 10
Processed Products 11-12
Delicious, Golden Delicious, McIntosh 13
Rome Beauty, Jonathan 14
Winesap, York Imperial. 15
Stayman, Newtown Pippin 16
Cortland, Gravenstein. 17
Rhode Island Greening, Northern Spy 18
Empire, Granny Smith, Mutsu 19
Simmer, Get Acquainted. 20
Taste Test, Composition 21
Drying, What You Need, Procedure 22
Dried Applesauce, Fried Apples,
Dried Apple Pie, Quantity Service 23
Microwave Cooking, Applesauce,
Apple Compote 24
Baked, Poached, Apple Arithmetic 25
Keeping Flesh White, Making Cider,
Making Pomace, Pressing Pomace 26
Canning, Freezing, Base For Jellies. 27
Spiced, Pie Filling, Apple Butter,
Chutney, Relish, Jelly 28
Jelly, Conserve, Relish 29
Comparing Varieties 30-32
Tools 33
Varieties and Uses. 34-35
Standard Apple Bird 36-37
Apple Birds .38-39

Stacked V's 40
Apple Spires. 41
Apple Plate .42-43
Grand Cheese Platter 44-45
Cheese Platter with Apple Wedges,
Stuffed Apples. 46-47
Eagle 48-49
Baskets 50-51
Coach 52-53
Twin Birds .54-55
Bird Of Paradise 56-57
3 Little Birds 58-59
Design Cutters. 60-61
Dove 62-63
Love Birds .64-65
Neptune's Pride 66-67
Flower 68-69
Goose 70-71
Mr. Peacock 72-73
Ms. Peacock 74-75
Shells 76-77
Swan 78-79
Turkey 80-81
Turtle 82-83

Outline Pattern-Fish 84
Outline Pattern-Love Bird 85
Outline Pattern-Auto 86
Outline Pattern-Coach 87
Outline Pattern-Eagle 88
Outline Pattern-Swan 89

Be Creative .90-95

Other Publications 96

"The apple is the loveliest of earth's fruits and we grow the best of them here in the United States. If it were the only fruit we had, it would be enough to satisfy body and soul. Born of the exquisite blossom whose faint pink and pure white make a vision of spring, it comes to maturity in autumn when the leaves are falling and the air has the sharp, fresh tang of the frost, the fulfillment of spring's promise of color, fragrance and beauty.

There is no flavor like that of a ripe apple, bursting with goodness. No cloying sweetness to fill the throat, no acid bits to pucker the mouth, no vapid flatness to disappoint the eager palate, is in an apple. Pure thirst-quenching juice soothes and flatters the taste, comforts the stomach, charms the spirit and contents the mind. Nothing that grows on a tree can compare with the apple.

It is the children's fruit, beloved of small boys for generations, cherished in the schoolbags of little girls with an eye on recess when it would be shared with the intimate friend, or given over to beloved teacher. Always it has been their first choice, their favorite and for good reason. It puts sparkle in their eyes, polish on their teeth, joy in their stomachs and health over all.

As for the grown-ups, it makes the great culinary triumph of these United States—apple pie. That in itself is enough to call for this hymn of praise."

—*Angelo Patri, M.D.*

Legends and Folklore

Apples are as old as mankind, and just as soon as man learned to write he began their recorded history. Many of our most fascinating stories, fables and legends are woven around apples. Was it an apple that tempted Adam in the Garden of Eden? The Bible doesn't say so, but down through the centuries we have credited the apple with man's downfall, probably because its superlative beauty and flavor would make it difficult to resist!

King Solomon, in his wisdom, hailed the apple as a fruit of healing. Ages later, in Devonshire, this saying arose: "Ate an apfel avore gwain to bed. Makes the doctor beg his bread." And today we claim, with substantial evidence to support it, that "an apple a day keeps the doctor away."

Greek and Roman myths abound in stories about the apple, symbol of love and beauty. Even today we refer to something or someone we prize as "the apple of our eye."

An apple was the cause of the Trojan War. It all began because Eris, Goddess of Discord, was miffed when she was not invited to the wedding of Peleus and Thetis. To avenge this snub, she had an artisan make an apple of solid gold, inscribed "To the Fairest." And on the day of the nuptials she tossed it among the guests. Three goddesses claimed it— Hera, Athena and Aphrodite. To put an end to their squabbling, Paris was called upon to judge what may have been the first beauty contest.

It appears that even goddesses were not above bribery. Hera promised Paris power and riches in return for the apple. Athena offered glory and renown as a warrior. But Aphrodite held out a reward no man could resist, the fairest of all earthly women for a wife—Helen of Troy. Unfortunately Helen was already married to Menelaus, King of Sparta, who failed to appreciate her abduction by Paris. So began a war that lasted ten long years!

It is said that when Zeus and Hera were married in the Garden of the Gods, a wonderful tree bearing golden apples sprang from the earth. These apples had "a taste of honey" and cured all illnesses.

Atalanta, beautiful goddess and huntress, was also fleet of foot. She challenged every man who sought her hand to a race, promising that if he won she would marry him, but if he lost, he must die. Because she was so beautiful, many men accepted the terms, and as many died, until one, called Hippomemes, bethought himself to pray to Aphrodite before the race. She answered his prayers by giving him three golden apples. Following her instructions, he dropped them, one by one, during the race. Each time, Atalanta was tempted beyond her strength and stopped to retrieve the apple, thus losing the race and winning a husband.

British folklore, too, is filled with praise of apples. An ancient Saxon coronation benediction reads, "Bless oh Lord the courage of this Prince and prosper the works in his hands and may this land be filled with apples."

In Herefordshire, Devonshire and Cornwall the old custom of "wassailing" the apple orchards on Christmas Eve still persists. The farmers walk in procession to a chosen tree in each orchard where an incantation is spoken and a bowl of cider dashed against the trunk of the tree, thus insuring a fruitful harvest.

Superstitions follow on legends, and in Devonshire this "cure" for warts may still be in use today: Halve an apple, rub it on warts, tie it back together again and bury it. The warts will vanish!

In Lincolnshire a poultice of rotten apples was once recommended for rheumatism. (Fresh apples in the diet would have been more effective!) And in Cornwall, in 1562, a clergyman treated every illness with a diet of apples and milk.

To go back to the Garden of Eden, most scholars agree that apples may well have originated in Southwest Asia, credited by Biblical savants as being the site of the Garden!

Carbonized remains of apples have been found by archeologists in prehistoric lake dwellings in Switzerland, going back to the Iron Age. There is also evidence to show that apples were eaten and preserved by slicing and sun-drying during the Stone Age in Europe.

In the earliest annals of China, Egypt and Babylon we find apples mentioned, and we know that man understood the art of budding and grafting fruit trees as long as twenty centuries ago.

When Caesar's Roman legions invaded Britain they introduced apples to those isles. Another Roman, Cato, who lived and wrote in the third century B.C., speaks of seven apple varieties, while Pliny, in the first century A.D., names 36 varieties. In the centuries that followed, apple orchards were planted all over Europe.

When the first settlers arrived in America they brought apple seeds with them. The first apple crop in the New World was harvested from trees planted by the Pilgrims.

In 1647 Governor Stuyvesant of New York (then New Amsterdam) brought a grafted apple tree from Holland and the trunk of this tree stood on the corner of Third Avenue and 13th Street until a dray knocked it down in 1866.

The first commercial apple tree nursery was established in Flushing, Long Island, in 1730.

When covered wagons lumbered over wilderness trails traveling westward, they carried apple trees and "scion wood" for grafting as part of their cargo.

Back East the Pennsylvania Dutch became expert at drying sliced apples, which they called "schnitz." They also made (and still make) fine cider, while their apple recipes have won renown for generations.

Farther South, in the Appalachian area, apple orchards were begun at about the same time as the New England plantings. George Washington and Thomas Jefferson were two famous apple growers in Virginia.

Today the annual apple crop in the United States is approximately 195 million bushels. Most of this fruit comes from 35 or more of the 50 states—states which offer a temperate climate, ample moisture and sunlight, well-drained soil, and a winter season during which the trees can rest.

Apples are produced around the globe. Australia, New Zealand, China, Japan, Israel, and many other nations of the Middle and Far East produce substantial volumes, while production continues in Europe and in the Americas.

Johnny Appleseed

Almost everyone thinks that Johnny Appleseed is the mythical hero of a charming American legend. Actually, this is the nickname of a real person, John Chapman, who was born in Massachusetts in 1774.

As a youth, John followed his father's trade of carpentry. He drifted away from his birthplace and eventually migrated to Pittsburgh. Here he listened avidly to tales about the pioneers who were trekking westward, and to stories of life on the frontier.

Ignoring the disdainful laughter of those in whom he confided, he ultimately set out alone with a sack of apple seeds gathered from a cider press refuse, an axe, a short-handled hoe and a Bible, to follow an urge to teach religion and to plant apple trees.

History

His possessions were few. Often he wore only a burlap coffee sack for clothing. Bareheaded and often barefoot, even when the weather was freezing, a saucepan on his head when it stormed, he traveled unarmed, often over the dangerous wilderness trails. Sometimes friendly Indians gave him moccasins. He was a welcome guest at homesteads where he stopped and he showed his appreciation by making toys for the children, by telling stories, and by reading aloud from his Bible.

Johnny Appleseed was a gentle man, a student of Swedenborgian philosophy. He never harmed a living thing, and had an almost mystical love of nature. Above all, he had a deep love and respect for all mankind, including the Indian tribes he encountered in his travels.

John Chapman, the beloved "Johnny Appleseed," died in the early spring of 1845 near Ft. Wayne, Indiana, while tending one of his numerous frontier apple nursery plantings. He was 71 years of age. A friend of everyone he met, an honored guest wherever he stayed, respected and beloved throughout the 10,000 square miles of frontier country he traveled, he is remembered today as one of that rare and truly good breed of men who devote their lives to their fellow men with no thought of reward.

Health and Nutrition

Ask everyone who is eating an apple, "What's so great about apples?" and you'll probably elicit a reply like, "They're great—I just like them, that's all." Press the question further and the respondent may elaborate, "because they're good...and good for you."

Enjoyment and good health...an unbeatable testimonial for nature's most nearly perfect fruit.

But what about the health and nutrition values of apples? What about the old "apple a day" adage; is it true?

Apples are a major member of the fruit and vegetable group of the four essential food groups which nutritionists recommend.

While apples are not a major source of any one specific nutrient they contain modest amounts of a number of the important nutrients. For this reason and their universal flavor appeal, versatility, convenience and year around availability, nutritionists and dietitians rate them highly.

Apples are low in calories, the food energy unit supplied by carbohydrates, fats and proteins. Apples are for slimming...one average apple supplies only about 80 calories. The energy that is supplied, however, comes from quickly available fruit sugars. Hence they meet one of the prime qualifications for snacks. They fill you up, not out, and provide quick energy.

Not all food and diet values can be measured in terms of precisely named nutrients. Apples, for example, provide bulk and fiber in the diet for the proper functioning of the body's digestive and regulatory systems. Pectin and hemicellulose and the acid and alkaline balance contribute to this. They are catalytic and contribute to fighting body toxins, aiding digestion and pepping up the entire body system.

Apples are an excellent source of pectin, which is associated with helping keep cholesterol levels in balance, a relationship felt to be significant in helping to prevent or reduce the dangers of coronary heart disease.

The relatively high potassium and low sodium ratio in apples is also significant in some cardiac and renal problems as well as in diets for overweight persons.

Studies have shown that persons eating apples regularly have fewer headaches and other illnesses associated with nervous tension; and also show a reduced incidence of colds and other minor upper respiratory ailments.

Apples are "Nature's Toothbrush." The mild fibrous texture of the apple for detergent action; its juice content; its delightful aroma and mouth-watering appeal to induce salivary activity, all combine to make the apple an ideal dentifrice and natural "toothbrush." Studies have shown a marked reduction in dental caries when apples are eaten regularly in lieu of or following excessive amounts of candies, pastries and other foods which leave sticky residues between and around the teeth.

While much research remains to be done to analyze and understand all the many ways apples contribute to better health and nutrition, the age-old adage, "an apple a day...," is true enough and is being more and more strongly confirmed.

People eat apples primarily for sheer enjoyment, but health and nutrition are important motivations too, and for good reason: They're the all around, year around health fruit and "glow" fruit. They are good for the teeth, the stomach, the skin and the complexion, the nerves, the smile and overall good health.

The Growing Of Apples

Apples do not reproduce "true" from seed. In other words, the fruit from a tree grown from the seed of an apple will not produce fruit quite like the apple from which the seed came. Thus, every apple seed produces a new variety. It is hardly surprising, then, that we have had 2,500, and more, different apple varieties mentioned in American horticultural literature. And these 2,500 were mostly from early Colonial days. Apple growers perpetuated a desirable variety by budding and grafting live buds from the tree bearing this fruit to a new seedling or another tree. Thus, wanted varieties could be grown for a much longer time than the life span of the original seedling tree. This is why we have apple varieties today that trace their ancestry literally from tree to tree—generation to generation—back to Colonial days.

Apple growing is a science called pomology. The perfect shape, beautiful color and distinctive flavor of each variety is not simply a matter of chance, but rather the result of the knowledge and efforts of many people.

Apple orchards need year-round care by trained people. The trees are planted 50 to 400 or more per acre, depending on the size of the tree at maturity.

Efficient management and care mean a better yield per acre, usually 600 or more bushels at harvest time. When there is a lavish bloom in the spring and a good "set" of fruit, some of the apples must be thinned out to give those remaining on the branches a chance to grow to a good size and take on good color.

Budding and grafting, planting, pruning, insect and disease control, pollination, irrigation and thinning are some of the many facets of the science and profession of apple growing. The orchardist must be a jack-of-all-trades and a master of them, too.

Harvesting, storing, packing and marketing are also vital factors in getting quality apples to the consumer in the best possible condition.

Apples and Hospitality

The fruit bowl has been a warm and friendly expression of hospitality almost since the beginning of recorded history.

Fresh fruit and cheese, long a standard final course on European menus, served after the "sweet," has become popular in America too.

Today the apple bowl and cheese tray have become a popular, sophisticated and delightful final course for lunch or dinner.

After a hearty meal when a rich dessert is often declined, a cold, crisp fresh apple with assorted cheeses provides a perfect final touch and satisfies without satiating. Simple to prepare, easy to serve, apples have a way of saying "We're glad you came and hope you'll come again."

Fresh apples are available the year around. They come ready to serve, colorfully packaged by Mother Nature in an assortment of varieties to satisfy every taste. Just refrigerate, then polish and serve when you're ready.

America's Favorite Pie—Apple

Pie is a favorite American dessert, and many regions have their own specialties, but the all-national top favorite, as proved by many surveys, is *apple* pie.

Who made the first apple pie, and when? No one seems to know for sure. We do know that pastry originated in the Golden Age of Greece and that the Romans carried home the recipe after conquering the Greeks. After that it traveled through Europe wherever the Romans went and was adapted to native customs and available foods.

In early times pies were heavy and hearty, usually served as a main dish. Chaucer wrote of a "coke" (cook) who could "well bake a pie," but in his day the ingredients in one pie would be marrow bones, sparrows, vegetables, nuts, dates, oysters, eggs, fruits, spices, wine, butter and sugar baked in a huge pan under a thick layer of pastry!

History

We do know that apple pie was in great favor as a dessert in the time of Elizabeth I, because it is mentioned in the literature of those years.

Oliver Cromwell, that fanatical Puritan who held sway in England in the mid 1600s, banned all pies throughout the Commonwealth because they gave people pleasure, and therefore must be wicked! When Charles II became king in 1660, his subjects not only welcomed him with enthusiasm but welcomed the return of their beloved pies as well!

Robert Oliver, in his book *An Apple A Day*, emphasizes the love of the English for apple pies. He tells a story about the Earl of Dudley, a multimillionaire who lived in the early 1800s and who "could not dine comfortable without an apple pie." Once, at a grand dinner party, he was greatly annoyed because no apple pie was served and kept up a steady, audible murmur: "God bless my soul! No apple pie."

Henry Mayhew, an English author, after interviewing thousands of London's "street people," published a book in 1851 called *Mayhew's London*. In it he writes of the "piemen" who once sold all sorts of small pies on the streets, including apple pie. He tells us that "pie shops" eventually almost destroyed their trade and that they then frequented summer fairs, races, public houses and taverns as the best sources of customers.

In colonial America, before the days of refrigerated storage, apples were peeled, cored, quartered and hung on cords in the kitchen to dry. These dried apples were used all winter long to make pies. From the moment apples were available, New Englanders ate apple pie for breakfast, and in some rural areas the custom persists. Once when Emerson was twitted about this, he asked, "What is pie for?"

In Colonial times pies were not beautiful or fancy, but they were good. The custom of baking pies in round, shallow pans rather than in deep square or oblong pans originated here for reasons of economy, in order to stretch scarce food supplies. Some cooks still insist that "take-off crusts" give apple pies an even better flavor. Sliced apples are arranged in a pastry-lined pie pan, and the top crust is laid on top, but not sealed to the undercrust. When the pie is done, the top crust is gently lifted off, sugar and spices are added, and the top crust put back in place.

In France, a fruit "pie" is round but has straight sides. The shell is made with pastry, and the fruit topped with a glaze. In Germany, what is called a fruit "kuchen" is made with a bottom crust of cookie-like pastry, filled with concentric circles of fruit, then baked and glazed. And so it goes—to each his own. But here in America we cling to our version: a two-crust apple pie baked in a round pan. Served warm, topped with a scoop of ice cream if you like, there is no dessert, however exotic, that can compare with it for superb flavor.

Apple Juice and Apple Cider

"Cider Apples"*
When God had made the oak trees,
And the beeches and the pines,
And the flowers and the grasses,
And the tendrils of the vines;
He saw that there was wanting
A something in His plan,
And He made the little apples,
The little cider apples,
The sharp, sour cider apples,
To prove His love for man.

Blended by nature into the 85% water content of apples are the unique and flavor imparting enzymes and aromas and essences of the apple which have made the juice of the adaptable apple a palate pleasing and thirst quenching beverage for thousands of years. Cider making is an art and science as old as the cultivation of apple trees.

Historically, apple cider in America, both sweet and "hard," began with the first harvest from orchards planted by the first colonists in Massachusetts and in Virginia. Until about 1930 apple cider was made and consumed in greater quantities than any other fruit juice in the United States. Now a resurgence of its popularity is renewing that number one ranking despite a greatly increased population and the introduction of many other fruit juices.

In colonial America and up to the mid-1800's, before canning and pasteurization and freezing were developed and generally used as methods of preservation, "hard cider" or fermented apple cider was the only fruit beverage in plentiful supply and universal and year around availability. Its production was much more of an art and science than simply letting nature and microbiology convert the flavorful juice of the apple into this palatable low alcohol beverage, and other more potent, brandy-like liquors.   *Author Unknown*

Early Colonists Produced Apple Juice and Apple Cider

History

Fresh sweet cider at that time, as now, was a very perishable product which in early America, without refrigeration, was very seasonal indeed. Carefully made, low alcohol (usually 4-7% alcohol) *hard cider,* or *cyder,* however, was the household beverage of the period which was enjoyed year around by the whole family, with meals and between meals. As with other otherwise good things, this pleasant and refreshing beverage in America fell into disrepute after opportunists increased its alcoholic content by various means, and *hard cider* lost its acceptance as the light and wholesome universal beverage it had been for generations.

Fortunately, pasteurization, canning and refrigeration soon came along to extend the seasonal availability of unfermented *sweet apple cider* and to introduce canned *apple juice.* So, while the misuse of *hard cider* created a reputation from which it is only now recovering, natural *sweet apple cider* and *apple juice* continue to be increasingly popular household beverages. Processing and packaging technologies provide an ever better product each passing year and today both are more popular than ever. And low alcohol *hard cider* too is recapturing much of its original popularity.

Buying and Handling Apples

In the retail food store apples are marketed in bulk, by the pound, in polyethylene bags of three, four, and five pounds, and in film-wrapped trays of two or more apples in each "over-wrap" or tray package.

Almost all apples are graded for marketing, and the package is identified with a U.S. Department of Agriculture grade of U.S. No. 1, U.S. Fancy, or U.S. Extra Fancy. Differences in grade are a matter of color, uniformity of size and shape, and minor superficial blemishes such as russeting, scratches and scars, which occur in production.

In selecting apples, check for bruising. Apples bruise easily, and a minor amount of bruising is almost impossible to prevent in shipping and handling. Bruises soon lead to decay, however, and excessive bruising usually means that the apples have been poorly handled and will decay more rapidly after you have taken them home.

Over-ripe apples, however, are not usually marketed, and you can feel reasonably secure in purchasing most apples on display.

They should appear bright and fresh looking. The green "ground color," or background color, when visible on varieties that are not a solid red color, should be a yellow-green. If too "grass green" in appearance, the apples may be too immature and will have a starchy, green taste. If the ground color is a faded yellow-green, the apples may be over-mature and will be soft and mealy with loss of juice and flavor. Today many apples are waxed to enhance appearance. The wax is safe and made with approved ingredients.

In storing apples at home, keep them cool. Whenever possible, reserve supplies should be refrigerated. Keep them in the hydrator or in the polyethylene bag in which you purchased them, to maintain proper humidity and to prevent them from absorbing other food flavors. Serve apples cold or at room temperature, as preferred.

Storage of Apples

The life cycle of an apple begins following fertilization and the start of a tiny green apple. From this moment on, its growth and development progresses to a peak point of optimum ripeness or maturity, then continues on the down side of the cycle until it finally spoils and decomposes.

Apples are harvested, as nearly as is possible and practicable, at optimum maturity. They are alive and continue to respire and age after being picked from the tree. The rate of respiration and maturation is directly related to temperature. The higher the temperature, the more rapid the rate of respiration and aging and the loss of optimum quality for eating. Apples kept at room temperature, for example, respire and age far more rapidly than they do in the refrigerator.

Because of their high water content, apples keep best in a reasonably moist atmosphere. A dry atmosphere tends to draw moisture from the fruit. Therefore the refrigerator hydrator is the best place to store them.

To preserve fresh apples and extend their availability for many weeks longer than their normal life span, huge refrigerators, or cold storages as they are called, are filled at harvest time each fall.

The first apple storages in America, back in Colonial days, and for many years thereafter, were called common storages or root cellars. They maintained temperatures above freezing, but were cool and moist. Late fall apple varieties, or "winter" varieties, could be kept in reasonably good condition all winter long in such storages.

The cellars of early American homes, with dirt floors, and later, concrete floors, provided excellent household storages for apples. Today, with the advent of central heating and dry, heated basements, this is no longer true.

One of the first American commercial cold storage facilities for apples was built in Niagara County, New York, in 1870. Ice, packed in sawdust, lining the walls, provided the first refrigerant. It was not until 1915 and thereafter that mechanical refrigeration took over.

While refrigeration extended the life cycle of a number of apple varieties, making them available for market for several months longer, February and March usually marked the end of the cold storage season.

In France, early in the 1800s, Jacques Berard, in research he was conducting, found that harvested fruits used oxygen and gave off carbon dioxide and that in an atmosphere largely or completely deprived of oxygen, they cease to ripen. He demonstrated that, if not totally deprived of oxygen, they were not suffocated and that the ripening process could be restored upon restoration of oxygen. While Berard's research was fifty years or more ahead of the practical and commercial development of mechanical refrigeration, it was the beginning of *Controlled Atmosphere Storage*. This type of storage reapportions the air in storage areas for apples in a way that slows the maturation rate to a point well below that of refrigeration alone and extends the crisp, flavorful life of fresh apples for additional months. With Controlled Atmosphere Storage fresh apples can now be kept, nearly harvest-time fresh, the year around.

In the late 1930's and early 1940's, Dr. Robert M. Smock at Cornell University pioneered controlled atmosphere refrigerated storage for commercial adaptation and the only controlled atmosphere storages in the United States were in eastern New York State, due largely to his intensive work. Currently, each year about 40 million bushels of apples, largely in New York, Michigan and Washington, but increasingly in all apple-producing sections of the U.S. and Canada, are stored in controlled atmosphere storages. This volume, plus many more in regular refrigerated storage, effectively "stretch" the apple season to year around availability. The apple truly is "The Fruit for All Seasons."

Processed Apple Products

Nearly one-half the apple crop in America each year is processed into convenient apple products: apple cider, apple juice, applesauce, canned and frozen pie-sliced apples, apple pie filling, whole baked apples, apple butter, dehydrated sliced apples and others.

Canned applesauce is the most popular and the most universally available processed product. It is packaged in number 10 size cans (approximately one gallon) for restaurants and other institutional users and in a range of consumer sizes of glass jars and cans. Applesauce is usually made from a blend of two or more apple varieties.

Canned pie-sliced apples and apple pie filling are also available in most food stores and are quick and easy to use for pies and other pastries, for toppings for ice cream and other desserts and many other uses.

Commercially prepared applesauce is usually not seasoned, because it would be too difficult to please everyone. However, it is an easy matter to "season to taste" and to experiment with many flavor combinations.

Apple juice, by itself and blended with other fruit juices, is increasingly popular and available year-round in all food stores. Sweet apple cider, fresh pressed at harvest time each fall, is still one of the most popular of all apple products. With refrigeration and freezing today, it is available for much of the year.

Know Your Apples

Varieties

It's fun to "know your apples"—and smart too—for full enjoyment of this delightful and versatile fruit is not to be found in any single variety, but in selection and choice for flavor enjoyment and cooking triumphs.

When it is understood that every seedling apple tree bears fruit that differs from every other seedling apple tree, the numbers of named varieties is not surprising. Of the millions of seedling trees that have produced fruit over the centuries, probably fewer than 8,000 produced fruit of such note that the variety was named, recorded and propagated. Of these, fewer than a thousand attained lasting recognition. Today, about fifty varieties represent most of the apple production throughout the world.

Nowadays nursery stock of apple cultivars from all over the world is shipped to all parts of the world. When America was colonized, only species of the wild crab apple were native to the New World. The apple as we know it came to America from Europe and to Europe from the Middle East. A comparative few of the best varieties were propagated for many generations and, indeed, are still produced today.

In 1872, Downing's *Fruits and Fruit Trees in America* listed and described over 1,000 named apple varieties of American origin.

The demands of present day mass marketing and food distribution, the need for large volumes of uniform and consistent supply, the preferences of the consuming public, the economic demand for high annual yields and efficient production of quality fruit that handles, stores and ships well—these and other reasons have eliminated most of the varieties of yesteryear.

It is now well over 300 years since the *Roxbury Russet*, one of the earliest known American cultivars, was first propagated. The *Rhode Island Greening, Winesap, Baldwin, Newtown Pippin* or *Yellow Newtown*, and others known in the early 1700s are still produced commercially today. And a number that were "discovered" at about the time of the Declaration of Independence and in the years prior to the Civil War, are still important commercial cultivars today: *Jonathan, McIntosh, Northern Spy, Rome Beauty, York Imperial, Grimes Golden* and others.

Many of the old favorites of the 1700's and early 1800's, however, like the *Roxbury Russet, Golden Russet, Black Gillflower* or *Sheepnose*; the *Bonum, Chenango, Pound Sweet, Esopus Spitzenberg, Winter Banana, Snow, Smokehouse, Wolf River, Sweet Bough*, and many, many others, while still produced, some even in limited commercial volume, are mostly produced only in "collectors' orchards"—for nostalgic reasons and hobby interests. The names of many of these bespeak the esteem in which they were held: *Seek-No-Further, Nonesuch*, and other superlative descriptive terms.

Horticultural history buffs delight in researching the origins or the names of the old varieties, many of which bear witness to historical events, places and names.

Even today, however, of the fifteen most important commercial varieties grown, only *Stayman, Delicious, Golden Delicious* and *Cortland* originated since 1850; and only *Cortland* is a product of the scientific plant breeder. All the others are of chance seedling origin.

Today, although most of the old chance seedling selections have gone, modern plant breeding and scientific evaluation and selection of apple cultivars to meet today's need are introducing many superb new selections. Modern commercial fruit farming has placed increased interest and emphasis on seeking out and propagating natural *bud sports* or mutations of major varieties that produce more highly colored fruit. Better yields, more efficient tree size and other growth characteristics are other factors that have accelerated the search for improved variations of all major varieties today.

A few of the many newer, scientifically developed hybrids, or crosses, of other varieties that are gaining popularity include *Empire*, a cross between *McIntosh* and *Red Delicious; Spartan*, a cross between *McIntosh* and *Newtown Pippin; Idared*, a cross between *Jonathan* and *Wagner; Jonagold*, a cross between *Jonathan* and *Golden Delicious;* and many others.

It's fun to "Know Your Apples"; exciting to know that this colorful, flavorful and versatile fruit keeps turning up in new and delightful varieties; and, best of all, fun to experience the many flavors and many wonderful ways to serve and enjoy all of them.

Delicious

Delicious, or *Red Delicious* as it is generally called, is the major volume variety produced in the United States, and an increasingly popular variety throughout the world. A chance seedling, it was discovered by Hiatt at Peru, Iowa, in 1872. He found it near an old *Yellow Bellflower* apple tree and because of this surmised that this variety may have been one of the parents. It was cut down twice because it was growing out of the row of other trees. Each time it sprouted up and grew more vigorously than before. Hiatt finally let it grow and bear fruit, and it was first named "Hawkeye." In 1895 Stark Brothers, a commercial nursery, purchased all rights to the variety and renamed it Delicious. This was one of the first varieties owned and marketed exclusively by a commercial nursery. Hiatt had won prizes with the "Hawkeye" at local horticultural shows. Stark Brothers' representatives first noticed it at one of these shows, and after some difficulty, located the owner and the tree and arranged for its purchase. Today there are more named color sports and strains and tree types of Delicious than of any other variety. Most of the Delicious production today is of these variously named sports of Delicious.

Golden Delicious

Is the *Golden Delicious* a direct descendant of the golden apple of Greek Mythology? We can't prove it, but it's a nice bit of fanciful conjecture! The Greek Gods would have cherished it.

Actually, it was discovered on the Anderson Mullin farm in Clay County, West Virginia, in 1914. Another chance seedling, careful research strongly indicates that it probably came from the *Grimes Golden* variety, pollenated by the *Golden Reinette* variety. Bearing trees of both of these old varieties grew near where the new seedling was discovered. The Reinette is of English origin and was also known as English Pippin. The Grimes Golden is of native West Virginia origin in the late 1700s. Fruit from the original tree of Grimes Golden was sold to New Orleans traders in about the year 1800 and the variety soon became highly prized for its delicate dessert quality and was planted extensively in the Appalachian area.

Fruit from this single seedling tree attracted considerable attention locally, both for its flavor and its excellent keeping quality. It was first called *Mullin's Yellow Seeding*. In the spring of 1914, Mullin sent some of the fruit to Stark Brothers Nursery. This nursery, looking for a companion variety for the already popular Delicious, soon purchased the Mullin's Yellow Seedling tree and renamed it Golden Delicious.

Today, it is the second major volume variety in the United States, a major variety in Europe, and increasing in popularity throughout the world. In the United States, the Golden Delicious is produced in nearly all of our apple-producing states, from Maine to North Carolina and from Virginia to the state of Washington. In Canada, too, it is grown to some extent in all apple-producing provinces.

McIntosh

John McIntosh was the youngest son of a Scottish family that emigrated to America about 1776 and settled in the Mohawk Valley of New York near Schenectady. John was born there in 1777. In 1796, following a disagreement with his parents, he left home and emigrated to Ontario, Canada. He operated a farm along the St. Lawrence River, and in 1811, exchanged farms with his brother-in-law, Edward Doran. It was on this farm, near what is now Dundela, Ontario, that the *McIntosh* apple had its origin.

John salvaged some young seedling apple trees that had grown up in the brush on a section of the farm and transplanted them to a garden area near his home. By 1830, only one of the transplanted trees had survived. The fruit from this tree, however, was greatly admired by the McIntosh family and all who sampled it for its aroma and spritely flavor. John planted seeds from the fruit and sold the seedlings to other settlers in the area. Like all seedlings, none resembled the parent tree. In 1835, however, a wanderer and peddler came through the area who knew how to graft and bud fruit trees. Out of this learning and experience John McIntosh developed an apple tree nursery and began propagating trees that now produced fruit identical to the parent tree. As his farming operation expanded, his wife, Hannah, took over the nursery, and as a result of this, the McIntosh apple was first called "granny's apple" by neighbors and fellow settlers who purchased trees at the McIntosh nursery.

A son, Allan, who continued the nursery business, named the variety McIntosh Red. A younger brother, Sandy, and Allan's youngest son, Harvey, continued the nursery and orchard in the years to follow. Relatives in New York and Vermont planted the variety and extolled its virtues. Through their interest as well as the nursery business itself, the McIntosh apple variety became well known and spread throughout the northeastern United States by the time the original tree, damaged by fire, finally died in 1910 after over 100 years of productive life and a three-generation nursery business dedicated to it.

The *Fameuse* or *Snow* apple variety, a popular variety in the 1700s and 1800s, has long been believed to have been one of the parents of the original seedling McIntosh. More recent horticultural scholars, sleuthing the possible origin of the variety, cite *Fall St. Lawrence*, and *Alexander*, as being two varieties grown in that area in the 1700s and early 1800s that may well have spawned the McIntosh. No one knows for certain.

Crosses of other varieties with McIntosh have created a number of new and promising hybrids, some already well known, including *Cortland, Spartan, Empire, Macoun, Niagara, Puritan* and many others.

McIntosh grows and matures to its crisp, juicy aromatic best in the cooler, late season apple-producing areas of the United States and Canada—around the Great Lakes and in New England states.

Ontario, Quebec, New Brunswick, New York, Michigan, Wisconsin and Minnesota all produce excellent McIntosh. Even in these states and provinces, however, the finest and best-colored fruit are produced where the temperatures remain coolest throughout the summer and fall.

Most aromatic of all our apple varieties, a bowl of McIntosh apples on a table imparts an orchard-fresh aroma to the entire house.

Rome Beauty

In the fall of 1816, a fruit grower, Joel Gillett, brought a number of young apple trees from Putnam's nursery at Marietta, Ohio, to a farm near Proctorville. (Putnam's nursery, started by Rufus Putnam in 1796, preceded by Johnny Appleseed's travels in the Ohio Valley country and included a number of eastern apple varieties for which Putnam

had brought scion wood from the colonies when he migrated west.)

The next spring, while preparing the trees for planting, Gillett discovered that one had sprouted from the seedling rootstock below the bud union which, of course, meant that it would not produce a tree of the variety he had selected. He discarded the tree and gave it to his son, Alanson, who planted it in the corner of a field away from the family orchard on the banks of the Ohio River.

Winning once more against the thousand-to-one odds which over the centuries had produced the comparatively few good varieties among the thousands of seedlings tried and discarded, this one produced such fine apples that it soon became a popular one for further propagation.

About the year 1832, a man by the name of George Walton named the apple *Rome Beauty*—for the Rome township in which the Gillett farm was located and Beauty because of its shape and attractive color. The original tree stood until about the year 1860 when it was washed away by the flood waters of the Ohio.

Like other major varieties, Rome Beauty has seen many more highly colored descendants which have been either mutations or hybridized crosses of Rome Beauty. *Gallia Beauty* is perhaps the best known bud or scion root sport of Rome Beauty. *Monroe*, a cross of Jonathan and Rome, *Ruby*, a cross of Gallia Beauty and Starking Delicious, are three of a number of the hybrid crosses with Rome Beauty parentage.

Rome Beauty is produced in very nearly all the apple producing states and provinces of the United States and Canada.

It became a popular commercial variety largely because of its long storage life and ease of handling without serious bruising, as well as for its attractive color and shape and large size.

Jonathan

A beautiful, brilliant red apple of excellent fragrance and flavor, the *Jonathan* variety was discovered at Woodstock, New York, in 1800. It was known locally as the Rick apple, after the name of the farmer, Philip Rick of Kingston, New York, who found it in his orchard.

Varieties

It was later renamed Jonathan, not because of Johnny Appleseed, as some have surmised and who was at that time in the midst of his missionary and apple planting travels in the Ohio Valley country, but rather after a man named Jonathan Hasbrouk, who, along with a Judge J. Buel of Albany, New York, first focused horticultural attention on this variety in 1826.

Jonathan is generally thought to have been a seedling of the popular old Esopus Spitzenberg variety, with the other parent unknown.

By 1845 this variety had received recognition by a number of eastern horticultural societies and was listed in a number of nursery catalogs.

In the first year of the Michigan Pomological Society, in 1870, Jonathan, already being grown extensively in Michigan, was extolled as a very choice apple, of excellent quality and a good keeper. Another major attribute of the Jonathan was that it was a very dependable annual producer.

In New York and in New England, the fruit tended to be small in size and the variety never became a major one for the area. In Michigan and the Ohio Valley area, in the Appalachian area and in the Northwest, it attains better size, color and finish. In the late 1800s and 1900s, it was the leading variety in Michigan and a major variety in a number of other states. Today, the important Jonathan states are Michigan, Ohio, Illinois, Missouri, Washington, Pennsylvania, the Virginias, Colorado and Idaho. Jonathan was the fourth ranking variety in the nation for a number of years and is still one of the top half dozen.

Jonathan has proved to be a great "parent" too, and modern plant breeding has developed a number of excellent new varieties using Jonathan as one of the crosses. A number of natural sports, also, have produced more highly colored fruits than the original tree found at Woodstock, New York.

It is one of the more difficult varieties to store, being susceptible to two or three postharvest conditions which limit its "keepability" in top quality and condition.

The advent of controlled atmosphere storage has been a boon for Jonathan, as it has for McIntosh, making both of these excellent varieties available for consumption during most of the year.

Winesap

Although it is one of our oldest and best known varieties and, for more than a century and a half, one of the most popular, probably less is known about the origin of *Winesap* than any of our other major varieties. Horticultural historians simply failed to record its origin. In 1817, William Coxe wrote that the Winesap was rapidly becoming "the most favorite cider fruit in West Jersey." This is the first early recorded reference to this variety. Because of this, the Winesap is generally believed to have originated in New Jersey prior to 1800.

The Winesap is a deep carmine red, moderately tart and rich in flavor. It is late-season variety, a good keeper, and for many years was the major variety available from late winter into spring and early summer.

With the advent of controlled atmosphere storage, which has made it possible to store many varieties for longer periods of time, the Winesap has declined in popularity and in supply.

Over the years it has been grown and marketed in all apple-producing sections of the United States and Canada. Today it is produced mainly in Washington, Virginia and West Virginia, with limited production in other states, including New Jersey, Pennsylvania and Indiana.

York Imperial

A variety much in demand for commercial processing, the *York Imperial* is not often found in the fresh produce departments of food stores. Chances are good, however, that you have enjoyed it when eating apple pie or applesauce at your favorite restaurant, or purchasing these processed apple products for home consumption.

Red color sports of this largely culinary variety have increased demand for it in the fresh market in recent years.

York Imperial was first discovered on a farm near York, Pennsylvania, about 1830. Children walking home from school in the early spring months discovered that "windfall" apples from a tree along the road, which had "hibernated" under snow and leaves all winter long, were mellow and crisp for eating.

Varieties

York Imperial, A Favored Variety For Processing

Johnson, who owned the farm and tree, took samples of the fruit to a local nurseryman, Jonathan Jessup, who began propagating and marketing trees of this variety, calling it *Johnson's Fine Winter Apple.* Jessup found little demand for the trees, however, and so discarded his supply of young budded trees in a hollow along the road. Farmers, returning home from market, salvaged some of the trees and planted them on their farms in southern York County. Thus, in this rather unpretentious way, this variety became better known and appreciated for its excellent keeping qualities as well as its culinary attributes, and soon became a popular variety throughout Pennsylvania, Virginia, West Virginia, Maryland and elsewhere.

Charles Downing, horticulturist and writer in the early and mid 1800s, examined some of the fruit, looked into its origin and history, and suggested that it be called York Imperial because of its origin and its ''imperial'' keeping qualities.

An active apple export business with England in the early 1900s gave the York Imperial the market demand it needed to utilize its increasing production.

British import restrictions in the early 1930s sharply changed the markets for apples in the Appalachian area. York Imperial, being a green apple, found tough competition with the more favored red varieties in the domestic market. But once again good fortune interceded, and the commercial processing industry, starting first as a kind of salvage operation, utilizing the smaller sizes and poorer grades of apples, gradually grew and expanded at about the time of World War II. York Imperial soon became a favored variety for processing.

The flesh of the York produces a much prized creamy yellow color in applesauce and canned sliced apples. It has excellent texture and holds its shape well when cooked. These qualifications, along with its good keeping characteristics, its small core and maximum yield of product, its firmness and resistance to bruising, all contributed to making it a top-rated variety for processing. In the early and mid 1930s several red color sports were discovered, which made it more competitive in the fresh market as well.

Stayman

This variety, grown throughout the Appalachian area, and to a lesser extent in the Midwest, originated as a seedling from the Winesap variety. The fruit is a less bright red than Winesap and is usually slightly russeted, particularly around the stem and blossom ends. It is marketed mainly in the Mideast and Midwest and is not as universally available as some of our other varieties. The *Stayman* was discovered and named by a Dr. J. Stayman at Leavenworth, Kansas, in 1866 and bore its first fruit in 1875. It is often called *Stayman Winesap* or *Stayman's Winesap.*

The Stayman didn't attract a great deal of attention until about 1890 when its good qualities were publicized concurrently by Mr. R.J. Black of Breman, Ohio, and Mr. J.W. Kerr of Denton, Maryland, two horticulturists of the time. Soon after 1900, it was planted extensively in the East and Midwest. Today it is an important variety for the fresh market and for commercial processing in southern Pennsylvania, the Virginias and Maryland, and is produced in limited quantity in New Jersey, Ohio, Missouri, Michigan, Indiana and a few other states.

Newtown Pippin

While the exact date and place of the origin of *Newtown Pippin* is not positively known, the original seedling is believed to have stood near a swamp on the estate of Gersham Moore, in Newtown, Long Island, New York. It died in 1805, an old tree, from excessive cutting of bud and scion wood. Its origin is believed to have been in the early 1700s, though no exact record exists, nor is it known whether the original tree was a *Yellow Newtown* or *Green Newtown.*

The Yellow Newtown (which is really yellow-green when mature) was considered the better apple for export and was far more extensively planted than Green Newtown.

Newtown Pippin, A Favorite Of Benjamin Franklin

Both varieties, also called *Newtown Pippin* varied considerably depending on the soil and climate where grown. In the 1800s the Yellow Newtown was grown extensively throughout most apple-producing areas of the U.S., doing best in the middle latitude areas of the country. Today it is grown almost exclusively in California and Oregon, with a few still produced in Virginia where it is known as *Albemarle Pippin,* having been so named for Albemarle County where it grows to perfection and where for many years it was felt to be a variety distinct from Newtown Pippin. It was later proved to have been started from scion wood brought to Albemarle County from Philadelphia by Dr. Thomas Walker in 1755.

The Newtown Pippin was the first American variety to be exported in volume to Europe, and the first American variety to be planted extensively in England, in contrast to the many European varieties planted in America. Thomas Jefferson and George Washington both planted this variety and Benjamin Franklin extolled its virtues in Europe.

Andrew Stevenson, as Minister to the Court of St. James in Queen Victoria's reign, had Albemarle Pippins shipped over from his farm in Albemarle County, Virginia, for his own use. He presented some of them to Queen Victoria, who was so delighted with them that she exempted this variety from a small tax which the Crown imposed on all imported apples. For many years thereafter the Albemarle Pippin, or Newtown Pippin, was by far the most popular apple exported from America to England. Today, nearly 200 years later, it continues to be one of our major export varieties; but now it is exported largely from Oregon rather than Virginia.

Cortland

Of the dozen or so major commercial apple varieties that account for most of our United States and Canadian production today, only the *Cortland* is the result of scientific plant breeding. All the others were chance seedlings or sports, selected and propagated from farm plantings or from untended trees in the wild.

Cortland was selected from among a number of carefully cross-pollinated hybrids at the New York State Agricultural Experiment Station at Geneva, New York, and named and introduced for commercial planting in 1915. It is the result of a cross between the McIntosh and the Ben Davis.

Cortland lacks the bright red color and spritely aroma of McIntosh, but has an attractive deep purple-red color of its own, and a greater resistance to bruising acquired from Ben Davis.

It is a superb eating and salad apple, having a snow-white flesh that does not darken as quickly as most other varieties when sliced or diced for salads and fruit cups.

Today the Cortland is produced largely in the areas where McIntosh is grown.

Gravenstein

This red-striped, moderately tart early fall variety is one of the few volume varieties in America introduced from Europe.

The origin of *Gravenstein* remains in doubt. Some say it originated in the Duke of Augustinberg's garden at Gravenstein, in Holstein, Germany, in the early to mid 1700s. Another account places its origin in the garden of the castle of Grafenstein in Sleswick, Germany. Others attribute its origin to Italy and its introduction into Germany and Sweden from that country.

Its first introduction to American orchards is also somewhat vague. Early horticultural writers make no mention of it prior to 1822. In 1857 a Captain DeWolfe stated that he had imported Gravenstein apples from Denmark in 1826. In a letter dated October 11, 1829, published in the *New England Farmer* magazine, Judge Buel of Albany, a prominent horticulturist and writer of that period, called attention to Gravenstein and other German varieties and presented trees to members of the Massachusetts Horticultural Society. The variety is generally credited as having been introduced in the Albany, New York, area prior to 1826. After these early importations, it was gradually planted in many other areas of the United States, including mission orchards in parts of California.

Varieties

The Russians planted Gravenstein and other varieties at Bodega, north of San Francisco, as early as 1820. Most early California plantings were begun about 1850. Thus the Gravenstein variety may have been planted in California before it was introduced to the eastern United States. Today, while grown in minor volume in a number of eastern states, most notably in New England and Delaware, the Gravenstein is largely a California product. In the Sebastopol area of California, it is the major variety for commercial processing into applesauce.

In Nova Scotia, Canada, Gravenstein and a red color sport of Gravenstein, called *Banks,* after a C.E. Banks of Kings County, Nova Scotia, who discovered it in 1880, are still grown quite extensively.

Rhode Island Greening

A highly rated culinary variety, the *Rhode Island Greening* is now produced largely in New York State and used mainly for commercial processing into canned and frozen apple slices and canned applesauce.

This variety is available in the fresh market at harvest time in the areas of production, but seldom marketed very widely.

The origin of the Rhode Island Greening is not known with certainty, but there is little reason to doubt early historical records, which place its origin in Rhode Island near a place known as Green's End in 1748. There a tavern keeper by the name of Green raised apple trees from seed and among the seedling trees he started was one that produced large green apples that were much in demand. Indeed history of the variety indicates that the original tree was ultimately killed from the extensive cutting of buds and scion wood!

The Rhode Island Greening was propagated in other New England states and New York in the mid 1700s. It was introduced into the old Plymouth Colony from Newport in 1765 and from there was carried to the state of Ohio in 1796 by General Putnam when he established a nursery at Marietta some years before Johnny Appleseed planted orchards in that frontier country.

Thus the Rhode Island Greening is one of our earliest known American varieties still being produced in commercial volume.

Northern Spy

The *Northern Spy,* or *Spy* as it is sometimes called, is a large, red, striped or blushed variety— tender, crisp and juicy, with a moderately tart, robust flavor. Highest in vitamin C of all our major American varieties, it is rated one of our finest dessert apples as well as a superb culinary variety. Apple pie made from Northern Spy is in a class by itself, while baked Northern Spy apples impart a flavor experience unequalled by any other variety.

The Northern Spy is produced mostly in New York, Michigan and Ontario, Canada, with small volumes in other northern states and provinces. In the areas of production it is available in late fall and early winter at roadside farm markets and to a limited extent in retail food stores; but the Spy today is utilized almost entirely for commercial processing where it is rated highly for frozen slices.

The Northern Spy originated as a seedling tree at East Bloomfield, New York, in an orchard planted in 1800 by Herman Chapin from seeds brought from Salisbury, Connecticut.

How it got its name is something of a mystery. Perhaps it was because it was discovered at the time when the "underground railroad," which secretly helped fugitive slaves escape to the northern states and to Canada in the years just preceding the Civil War, was in operation. One of the escape routes led through the area in the vicinity of Bloomfield to Sodus Point on Lake Ontario.

The original seedling tree died before bearing fruit, but suckers growing up from the base of the tree were transplanted by a Roswell Humphry, and he produced the first Northern Spy apples.

The Spy was propagated locally in western New York for many years before it attracted the attention of horticulturists in other areas. In about 1840, its qualities were more widely publicized. In 1852 the American Pomological Society listed it as a variety of considerable promise and worthy of general cultivation. By the turn of the century it was extensively planted in the more northern fruit areas of the Northeast, the Great Lakes States and Canada. Today, while it is an important variety in New York, Michigan and Northern Ontario, Canada, it has declined in most other areas.

Granny Smith, A Hard, Tart Snack Apple

Varieties

The Spy has a strong tendency to bear crops only in alternate years and is a late starting variety, often taking seven to ten years to begin to bear crops. For these two major economic reasons, despite its premium quality as a dessert apple and as a processing apple, Northern Spy has declined in popularity and is not currently being extensively planted. It was not until the Delicious variety was discovered that growers and horticulturists began to look seriously for bud sports of all apple varieties. For nearly 100 years no sports of Northern Spy were reported. In the 1920s and thereafter a number were found and named, but none has ever really equalled or exceeded the quality of the original Northern Spy; and none to date has overcome the biennial bearing and slow starting characteristics of the original variety.

Northern Spy is one of the parents of a number of scientifically bred hybrids that are being planted and tested at the present time in the United States and Canada. It is too early to judge these latest introductions as yet; but, again, while Northern Spy transmits many excellent characteristics, it seems to keep its finest attributes—its flavor and crisp, juicy composition—to itself. It may be that, like fine wine, the long years to bearing age and the biennial bearing characteristics of Northern Spy are the price exacted for its excellent quality.

Empire

A McIntosh type apple only with brighter, nearly solid carmine red coloring as contrasted with the more typically two toned red and green coloring of the McIntosh, the Empire is the result of a cross between the McIntosh and the Red Delicious varieties. It is a little sweeter than the McIntosh, but not that of the Delicious, and compromises a little of the juiciness of the Mac for more of the texture of Delicious. It is a popular, comparative newcomer to the world of apples, originating at the New York Agricultural Experiment Station, Geneva, New York, introduced for commerical production in 1966.

The Empire grows well wherever the McIntosh is grown. It is an excellent keeping variety; is an excellent flavored fresh eating apple for snacks and fruit cups and salads, but only fair for cooking and baking.

Granny Smith

While a relative newcomer to U.S. apple lovers, this tart, spritely, bright green variety has been a world wide favorite for well over a hundred years and ranks among the top five varieties in world production volume.

Granny Smith had its origin in Australia in 1868. Marie Ann (Granny) Smith and her husband Thomas first discovered this apple on a seedling tree growing by chance at the edge of their small orchard near Sidney, Australia. They liked its sprightly flavor and other qualities, as did others who sampled it. More trees were budded from the original volunteer tree, and gradually the variety has circled the globe.

Granny Smith requires a very long growing season for proper maturity and thus is grown in those areas of the world where such a season will accommodate it. In the U.S. it is grown largely in California, Washington, Arizona, and to a lesser extent in most others of the more southern apple growing states.

In the U.S. the Granny has enjoyed a rapid growth of popularity as a hard, tart snack apple since being "discovered" in the mid 1970's. It is also an excellent cooking and baking variety.

Mutsu

This Golden Delicious type variety from Japan was introduced for commercial production in the U.S. in 1948, the same year that it was introduced at home by the Japanese Horticultural Association.

The Mutsu is the off-spring of a cross between the Golden Delicious and a Japanese variety, Indo. It is a comparatively large yellow green apple, with some of the characteristics of each parent. It is a little more tart than the Golden Delicious, is a good keeper, and popular for snacks and salads as well as most culinary uses.

To date it is being grown mostly in the northeast U.S. where it grows fairly russet free as compared to the Golden Delicious which often russets extensively in the more moist climate of the eastern U.S. as compared to the more arid west.

All Apples Are Not Created Equal...

Other Varieties

Quite a number of other varieties are popular in different apple producing regions of the country, but are not produced in sufficient volume for more universal distribution.

A number of newer varieties too are gaining in popularity in the market today. Those who are fortunate enough to visit the many roadside or retail farm markets in the United States and Canada often have the opportunity to see and sample some of these long before they become available in the metropolitan areas.

Simmer, Don't Boil

All apples are not created equal! Each variety has its own unique flavor; only you can decide which is best. While all apples are nutritious and good to eat fresh, out of hand, some varieties tend to hold their shape much better throughout the cooking process. Generally speaking, the apple varieties that mature late in the season (after September) are better for cooking. Some of these include in no particular order of preference:

Golden Delicious	Jonathan
Cortland	Newtown Pippin
Northern Spy	R.I. Greening
Rome Beauty	Winesap
York Imperial	

Keep your apples cool to keep them crisp and fresh. Apples ripen about ten times faster at 70° F. than at 32° F. Store them in plastic bags or in the vegetable crisper section of your refrigerator to preserve their moisture. Take out only enough to serve your needs each day.

To keep apple slices from browning in the air, brush on or dip the slices in a bath of 1 part lemon juice to 3 parts water. You can also use a solution of 2 tablespoons each of salt and vinegar per quart of water, as a substitute for lemon juice. Hold slices in this solution no more than 10–15 minutes, then remove them and drain. Ascorbic acid (Vitamin C) may also be used for the same purpose.

When cooking overripe or bland-flavored apples, you can intensify by using apple juice or cider as the cooking liquid. Overripe apples tend to mush when cooked. Rapid cooking also causes apples to mush or fall apart. Shape is better retained when apples are simmered, not boiled. Cooking should stop as soon as the apples are tender. The "stop cooking" point is more critical with varieties such as McIntosh and Cortland than with apples of a firmer texture.

Like other fruits, apples tend to keep their shape better when cooked in a syrup. If the apple is quite firm, it's a good idea to cook it in water for a minute or two to soften it before adding the sugar. This helps speed up the sugar penetration.

You can save some energy when the oven is on and there is room to spare by adding a pan of apples. Baked apples aren't fussy about temperature. They bake beautifully in temperatures from 250° F. to 400° F.

Get Acquainted With Apples

Like people, apples present an infinite variety of appearances and personalities. Differences in varieties are due to genetic factors. Shape and color make them identifiable by sight. For instance, Rome Beauty is round and voluptuous. Red Delicious is elongated, with five points at the blossom end. Apples may be round, oval or, like York Imperial, lopsided. They come in all sizes, and their colors vary from warm light red to deep burgundy; from pale yellow to bright green; or, like McIntosh, two-toned, both red and green.

Factors which determine taste are sugar, acid and certain aromatic ingredients. As apples mature, enzymes change the starch into fruit sugars. The degree of tartness depends on the amount of mallic acid present, while the sweetness depends mainly on the content of fructose, a type of sugar that also gives honey its sweetness.

Aroma is a complex matter; over 50 different compounds have been identified in the essence of some apple varieties. Attempts to duplicate the apple essence for the perfume industry have thus far not proved practical. Some of the volatile aromatic compounds found in low concentration are responsible for the characteristic flavor of apples. Density and texture also differ between varieties; however, this is not a reliable character feature because the texture of all apples changes considerably as they ripen.

How To Do an Apple Taste Test

Apple taste testing is one way to really learn the subtle differences between apple varieties. Just as wine and cheese tasting parties have heightened people's awareness and interest, apple taste testing can provide an entertaining experience that your guests will long remember. You can offer a brief description and history of each variety and conducting an identification quiz adds fun and interest to the apple testing. Serve apple drinks, cheese and nuts to complement the theme, and an apple dessert to highlight the event.

Apple Taste Test

Three or more varieties are needed for comparison. Use a large plate for each variety.

1. Place one whole apple, and cut-up pieces of another apple of the same variety, on each plate.

2. Look at the whole apple. Note size, shape, color and stem.

3. Look at cut apple. Note flesh color: White? Creamy? Yellow? Is peel thin? Thick? Smooth? Leathery?

4. Smell each apple. Does it have a characteristic aroma?

5. Taste a slice of each variety. Is it sweet? Tart? Sour? What about texture–is it tender? Crisp? Juicy? Mealy? Hard? Is the peel tender or tough?

6. Which variety has the most flavor? Which has the strongest aroma?

7. Note the color of the slices after exposure to air. Does the flesh of some varieties stay white longer?

8. Which varieties would be best for salads and fruit cups? Which would go best with meat? Which for desserts?

9. Which varieties would combine best to flavor pies and sauces?

10. Which variety do you prefer to eat fresh, out of hand?

Composition and Nutritive Value of Fresh Apples

One medium apple about 2½ inches in diameter weighs about 150 grams (⅓ pound) and supplies approximately 85 calories of food energy. Nutritive values listed per 150 gram, unpeeled fresh apple. Source: U.S.D.A. Agriculture Handbook No. 8.

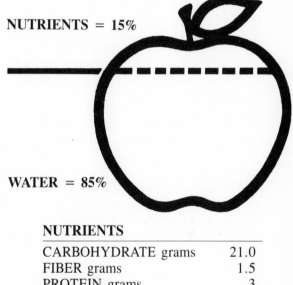

NUTRIENTS = 15%

WATER = 85%

NUTRIENTS

CARBOHYDRATE grams	21.0
FIBER grams	1.5
PROTEIN grams	.3
FAT grams	.9
ASH grams	.45
PECTIN grams	1.2*

MINERALS

CALCIUM milligrams	10.5
PHOSPHORUS milligrams	15.0
IRON milligrams	.45
POTASSIUM milligrams	165.00
SODIUM milligrams	1.5
MAGNESIUM milligrams	12.0

VITAMINS

A international units	135.0
THIAMIN (B) milligrams	.04
RIBOFLAVIN (B) milligrams	.03
NIACIN milligrams	.15
C (Ascorbic Acid) milligrams	6.0

*From other sources.

Drying Apples

Of all the methods of preserving food, drying in the sun is the simplest and most natural and oldest. It is also the least expensive, requiring little more than cutting the apples into small pieces and spreading them in the sun. Dried foods take up little space and can be stored in almost any air-tight container in a cool, dark place. A number of excellent books have been published in recent years and anyone interested in drying foods should check their local library.

Centuries ago, the American Indians preserved their fruits, vegetables and meats for the winter by drying them in the sun. Today there are many who believe that sun drying is the best way to preserve natural goodness in foods.

In 1769, St. John de Crèvecoeur, a surveyor-farmer in New York state, described how apples were peeled, sliced and hung on strings-to dry in the sun.

"They were soon covered with bees and wasps and sucking flies of the neighborhood," wrote Crèvecoeur. "This accelerates the operation of drying. Now and then they are turned. At night they are covered with blankets. If it is likely to rain, they are gathered and brought into the house. This is repeated until they are perfectly dried...

"It is astonishing to what small size they shrink," he went on. "The method of using them is this. We put a small handful in warm water overnight; next morning they are swelled to their former size; and when cooked either in pies or dumplings, it is difficult to discover whether they are fresh or not."

Fortunately, apples are one of the easiest of all foods to preserve by drying. You can use the sun, or your kitchen oven. The pilot light or light bulb in your oven will adequately dry thin apple slices within 24 hours. Using the sun as heat requires 3 to 4 sunny days.

When to Dry

Oven drying may be tried at any time, but with the sun, the only practical time for a serious effort is at apple harvest time in September or October. The apples are fresh and plentiful; the sunlight is still adequate in most of the United States.

What You Will Need

1. Shallow trays, cookie sheets or a set of wood-framed screens, as illustrated. Note: Make frame size 2 inches less than your oven size and alternately stack screen at 90 degrees to provide for complete air circulation while drying.

¾ " x 1 " pine frame
held with 1 ½ " brads

Aluminum screening
or hardware cloth
stapled to frame.

DRYING FRAMES are stacked alternately at 90° to provide complete air circulation.

2. A place in the sun (or an oven). A low roof or porch near the kitchen is ideal—the ground is too accessible to pets and insects. A cold frame sash reduces drying time considerably by concentrating the sun's heat, while the glass keeps bugs and animals out.
3. A screen or cheesecloth cover to keep out flying insects.
4. Fresh apples. Select firm, mature fruit.

Procedure

1. PREPARE THE APPLES. Peel, core and remove all bruises. Cut into small slices ⅛-inch thick and drop into cold water that contains 4 tablespoons each of salt and cider vinegar per quart (to retard browning of apples). Soak slices no more than 15 minutes.

Prepare one tray at a time and spread slices one slice deep on screen racks, or cloth-lined trays if metal trays are used.

Place in the hot sun or an oven with a temperature range of 105° F. to 150° F. maximum. The ideal drying temperature for best vitamin retention is 120° F. Set the trays on your kitchen counter if you want to use the oven to cook dinner, and replace the trays when the oven has cooled to below 150° F. Stir or turn slices a few times a day to promote uniform drying. When using the sun you can continue the drying process by using your oven at night.

Recipes

2. TEST FOR DRYING EACH DAY. Apple slices will be dry when the moisture content is reduced to 5% to 25%.

TO TEST: Cut a slice in half. Squeeze halves together. If sufficiently dry, no moisture will be pressed out. Roll a slice tightly in your hand. If dry, the slice will uncurl slowly when released. It will not crackle or break. It will feel pliable and leathery. Be sure all slices have dried.

3. STERILIZE BEFORE PACKAGING. Spread dried apples on metal trays or pans and heat in oven at 180°–200° F. for 15 minutes. Allow slices to cool before packaging.

4. PACKAGING: Dried apple slices may be safely stored in any container that protects them from moisture and insects. Tightly sealed plastic bags or glass jars are fine. Small packages will permit you to open and use up the contents without exposing the remainder to humid air. Air contact can be minimized by packing jars tightly. When sealing plastic bags, air contact can be reduced by sucking the air out of the bag with a soda straw before sealing.

Date and label all packages and store in a cool dry place protected from light as much as possible. Light will fade dried fruits. Properly packed and stored, your dried apples will keep safely for at least one year.

Cooking With Dried Apples

When you dried apples you removed the water. To restore the apples you put back the water. This is accomplished by soaking.

Baked beans are one of the most familiar dried food recipes. Most people know you soak the beans overnight, then cook them for several hours. Dried apples are prepared the same way. Soak the apples overnight in warm water. In the morning, drain them and use in your recipe. Allow a minimum of 6 cups of water for each pound of apple slices when soaking.

Dried Applesauce

Dried apple slices may be cooked without soaking if they are simmered over low heat 2 to 3 hours. Add water as needed. Keep covered and stir occasionally. Season with a little lemon juice and add ½ cup of raisins to each 2 cups of apples.

Fried Apples

Soak ½ pound of dried apple slices overnight in 3 cups of boiling water. Drain and fry lightly with breakfast bacon. Serve hot with bacon and eggs.

Dried Apple Pie

Cover 1½ cups dried apples with 3 cups water and simmer over low heat until tender. Add ½ cup sugar, 1 teaspoon dried lemon peel. Pour into unbaked pie shell and dot with butter. Sprinkle with ½ teaspoon ground cinnamon. Cover with top crust. Bake in 350° F. oven 30 minutes, or until brown.

Quantity Service

Recipes can be easily adapted for quantity service by a simple process of multiplication. In other words, you can double, triple, etc. your ingredients using these equivalents.

3 teaspoons = 1 tablespoon	2 pints = 1 quart
16 tablespoons = 1 cup	4 quarts = 1 gallon
1 cup = 8 fluid ounces	1 1-pound can = 2 cups,
2 cups = 1 pint	approximately

For other special recipes for foodservice, write to International Apple Institute.

Recipes

Microwave Cooking With Apples

Microwave ovens have become a popular appliance in many homes. And deservedly so; when used according to directions, significant savings of time and energy can be realized, as foods cook from two to four times faster with a microwave than with a conventional oven. However, microwave cooking calls for a change in cooking procedures, and each cook must be guided by the manufacturer's instructions and schooled by personal experience with the brand of oven used.

Most of the recipes in this book are ideal for microwave cooking. The exceptions are those where, for instance, a recipe calls for browning and your oven does not have a browning element. For foods that need to absorb water–pastas and rice, for example–you have to allow the same amount of time in the microwave oven as you do when cooking conventionally.

Cooks who freeze apple pies will find that the microwave oven saves considerable time if the pie is baked before freezing. It will thaw and reheat in ten minutes. Note, of course, that the manufac-turer's instructions must be followed on the use of proper containers in microwave cooking.

Microwave cooking time is directly related to the size amount, starting temperature and density of the food. One small apple requires slightly less cooking time than one large apple. As you place more items in the oven you must allow more cooking time.

The first microwave ovens on the market differ considerably in cooking time and features from those available today. And like most new household appliances, new features are introduced frequently so it's impossible to offer standardized recipes for all models. The instruction books accompanying ovens offer helpful suggestions for converting your own recipes. Many electric utility companies have home economists who can also help you.

The following recipes may be used as a guide to adapt other recipes in this book to your oven. These recipes illustrate the difference between conventional and microwave cooking. Note: the examples used are based on a 600-watt microwave oven.

APPLESAUCE

2 pounds apples	½ cup sugar, or to
½ cup water	taste (optional)

Wash and quarter apples. Discard stems and blossom ends.

Conventional Range

Combine apples and water in heavy saucepan. Cover, bring to a boil and simmer over low heat, stirring often, 15 to 20 minutes, until tender.

Microwave Oven

Combine apples and water in 3-quart bowl. Cover, cook 8 to 10 minutes, stirring halfway through cooking period.
Cooking Time Saved: 10 minutes
Force fruit through a sieve or food mill. Add sugar to taste while hot. Cooking time depends on variety of apple used. Makes 6 servings.

APPLE COMPOTE

2 firm ripe apples	½ cup honey
12 ounces dried	½ cup white wine
mixed fruit	Hot water to cover
1 orange	

Peel and core apples, cut into bite size pieces. Arrange with dried fruit in a large shallow baking dish: Peel and grate rind of orange over fruit. Section the orange and add. Pour the honey over all, add wine and water to cover.

Conventional Oven

Bake at 350° F. for 1 hour, until fruits are tender, stirring occasionally.

Microwave Oven

Cook until fruits are tender, about 15 minutes, stirring once or twice during cooking.
Cooking Time Saved: about 45 minutes.
Makes 8 serving.

The Microwave Saves Time And Energy...

Recipes

BAKED APPLES

4 baking apples	3 tablespoons chopped
3 tablespoons butter	walnuts
⅓ cup brown sugar	¼ cup apple juice or
3 tablespoons raisins	water

Core apples. Combine butter and sugar, add raisins and nuts and stuff into cavity of apples.

Conventional Oven

Arrange in shallow dish, pour 1 tablespoon of apple juice or water over each apple. Bake at 350° F. for about 40 minutes, until tender. Place on serving dish, spoon sauce over fruit.

Microwave Oven

Place apples in individual serving dishes, pour 1 tablespoon of apple juice or water over each apple. Cover with wax paper. Cook 8 minutes, until tender.
Note: 2 apples cook in 4 minutes.
Cooking Time Saved: 30 minutes.
Exact cooking time will depend on variety and size of apples. Makes 4 servings.

POACHED APPLE RINGS

3 large apples	Confectioners'
3 tablespoons butter	sugar
or margarine	2 tablespoons water,
	apple or lemon
	juice

Wash, core and cut apples into ½-inch-thick rings.

Conventional Range

Heat butter or margarine in a large skillet, add apples in a single layer. Sprinkle with sugar to taste, add water or juice to pan, cover and poach gently until tender, about 12 minutes.

Microwave Oven

Melt butter or margarine in large shallow dish, about 30 seconds. Add apples in a single layer. Sprinkle with sugar to taste. Add water or juice to dish. Cover with wax paper, cook 5 minutes, until tender, rotating dish ¼ turn halfway through cooking.
Cooking Time Saved: 7 minutes
Exact cooking time will depend on variety and size of apples. Makes 6 servings.

Apple Arithmetic

U.S. and Metric Measures

3 medium-size apples equal 1 pound or ½ kilogram.
Pared and sliced, 1 pound apples yields 2¾ cups, 4.3 ounces or 122 grams.
3 pounds apples equal 1.4 kilograms or 1,360.8 grams.
4 pounds apples equal 1.9 kilograms or 1,814.4 grams.
5 pounds apples equal 2.3 kilograms or 2,268.0 grams.
A peck of apples weighs 10.5 pounds or 4.76 kilograms or 9 liters.
A bushel of apples weighs 42 pounds or 19.04 kilograms or 35.238 liters, dry measure.
A bushel of apples will yield 15–20 quarts of applesauce or 11.4 to 15.1 liters.

Can sizes for fruit most commonly available and the approximate amounts:

Net Weight or Volume	Approximate Contents	Metric Measure
Fruits:		
8½ or 8¾ ounces	1 cup	226.8 grams
16 or 17 ounces	1¾ to 2 cups	453 to 468 grams
20 ounces	2¼ to 2½ cups	567 grams
29 ounces	3¼ to 3½ cups	850 grams
Juices:		
6 fluid ounces	¾ to 1 cup	170.1 milliliters
12 fluid ounces	1½ cups	340.2 milliliters
1 pint	2 cups	.473 liters
1 quart, 32 ounces	4 cups	.946 liters
3 quarts	12 cups	2.85 liters
1 gallon	16 cups	3.8 liters

APPLE SIZES: The diameter or size of apples range from 2¼ inches in diameter, or 57.15 millimeters, to 3⅞ inches or 99.03 millimeters. The most popular sizes are 2⅞ inches (73.63 millimeters) to 3⅛ inches in diameter (76.376 millimeters).

Apple Cider... The Common American Beverage

Recipes

Keeping The Apple Flesh White

When an apple is cut, the exposed flesh surfaces in most varieties rather quickly turn brown. To retard browning or discoloration of the exposed apple flesh surfaces, coat (or spray) with lemon juice. A number of commercial anti-oxidant products are available on the market for this purpose.

The flesh of some apple varieties stays whiter longer naturally when exposed to the air...Golden Delicious and Cortland for example, but even these will begin to discolor after an hour or two if not treated with lemon juice or an anti-oxidant product.

Making Apple Cider At Home

Throughout history, apple cider both sweet and low alcoholic cider has given pleasure to each age. In early America, apples and cider added zest and satisfaction to the arduous task of settling the wilderness.

John Adams, our second president, drank a tankard of cider every morning before breakfast until the end of his ninety-one years. In country inns and taverns cider was the common breakfast drink. College students were usually served cider with all meals. For nearly three hundred years apple cider was the common beverage of Americans.

Making Cider

Cider making is simply a process of separating the apple juice from the apple. Although the process is simple, considerable physical work is required if a quantity of cider is wanted and power machinery is lacking. For those who have the desire and perhaps a little ingenuity, in lieu of professional equipment the following items will permit you to produce your own supply of sweet cider.

Wine press	Scrub brush	Cheesecloth
Slaw slicer	Food chopper	Two pails
Scoop	Wood bowl	Glass jugs

First, wash everything, including the apples. A bushel or two of apples may be washed and scrubbed in the kitchen sink. Be sure to clean around the stems and blossom ends. If several bushels or more are to be washed, they may be piled on a large cloth on the ground and washed under the full pressure of water from a garden hose.

Making Apple Pomace

Grinding, grating, slicing or chopping the apples, after washing, into fine mush or pomace will produce the most juice with the least amount of pressing. A slaw cutter, one of our oldest kitchen tools, still works well for small batches; however, the new electric food choppers take all the drudgery out of the operation. Slicing and chopping in a wood bowl can be done but more time is required.

Pressing The Pomace

Small wine presses are suitable for pressing small batches of apple pomace. The press consists of a cage to hold the pomace and a screw device that is turned to squeeze the pomace. Consult the yellow pages of your telephone directory under the heading "Wine Makers' Equipment and Supplies."

To begin the pressing, line the cage with cheesecloth or cotton sheeting to form a bag. The pomace is scooped from a pail into the cloth. A second pail is placed under the drain spout of the press, with several layers of cheesecloth tied over the top of the pail to strain the juice as it runs from the press.

When the cage of the press has been filled with pomace, the excess cloth is folded over the top and the screw turned to begin the pressing. The pressing is done slowly, in stages, to get the maximum yield of juice. Pressure is applied and the juice begins to flow. When the flow subsides, more pressure is applied and the process continued until the last drop has been squeezed.

Preserving

With all the fine processed apple products available at groceries and supermarkets, home canning and freezing may not be in wide practice nowadays. But for those who delight in their own apple trees, and cannot bear to waste any of the lovely fruit, directions may be helpful. 'And it's fun, too, to see rows of glasses holding sparkling, colorful jellies, jams and conserves, made in the home kitchen.

How To Can Apples

Make light or medium syrup in amount needed, using 2 cups sugar to 1 quart water to yield 5 cups light syrup, or 3 cups sugar to 1 quart water to yield 5½ cups medium syrup.

Wash, drain, core, pare and slice cooking apples (or cut into halves or quarters), dropping prepared apples immediately into an ascorbic acid and citric acid solution made according to manufacturer's directions, to keep apples from discoloring. Or add 2 tablespoons each salt and vinegar to 1 gallon of water. If the latter solution is used, do not leave apples in it longer than 20 minutes, and rinse well before packing.

Boil drained apples in syrup 5 minutes. Pack, hot, into hot jars, leaving ½-inch head space. Cover with boiling syrup, leaving ½-inch head space. Add ascorbic acid and citric acid mixture according to manufacturer's directions. If pure ascorbic acid is used, sprinkle ¼ teaspoon over fruit in each quart jar before capping.

Adjust caps according to manufacturer's directions. Process pints and quarts for 20 minutes in boiling water bath. Complete seal, if necessary. Cool upright, away from drafts.

How To Can Applesauce

Wash, quarter and core apples. Add just enough water to prevent scorching; cook over low heat 15 to 20 minutes, or until tender. Put through food mill or sieve. Add sugar to taste; heat until sugar dissolves. Bring to boiling point. Pack boiling hot applesauce in hot sterilized jars, leaving ½-inch head space. Partially seal; process 5 minutes in hot water bath. Be sure to keep water at least 1 inch above tops of jars. Cover kettle; bring to boil. Begin counting processing time as soon as water starts to boil. Keep water boiling constantly. When processing time is up, remove jars to a cooling rack or folded towels, out of drafts. Complete seal immediately. Self-sealing jars do not need tightening. When jars are cool, wipe off the outside, and label. Applesauce may be spiced to taste before canning, but many authorities feel that flavor is improved if applesauce is canned without spices and these seasonings added when the jar is opened for serving.

How To Freeze Apples

Select firm, tart apples. Core, pare and slice into a brine made with 2 tablespoons salt to 1 quart water. Prepare sugar syrup, using 1 cup sugar to 2 cups water. Add ½ teaspoon powdered ascorbic acid to each quart of syrup, to prevent discoloration. Drop drained apple slices into simmering syrup (180°); simmer 3 minutes. Cool quickly. Pack apple slices with syrup in which they were cooked, leaving head space of ½-inch for pint containers, ¾-inch for quart containers. Seal. Freeze at once.

How To Freeze Applesauce

Prepare applesauce but, if spice is used, increase amount by about ¼, as flavor lessens during frozen storage. Cool quickly. Package, seal, label, freeze at once.

How To Freeze Apple Pies

Unbaked: Do not slit the top crust. To bake, slit top; place, frozen, in 425° oven; bake 40 to 60 minutes.

Baked: Cool thoroughly before freezing. To bake, place frozen, in 375° oven; bake 30 minutes.

Apple Juice Base For Jellies

Cut 4 pounds (3 quarts) tart apples into quarters. Do not pare or core. Add 2 quarts water. Cook 20 to 30 minutes, or until apples are tender. Strain through a dampened jelly bag. Makes about 6 cups juice.

Apple Condiments Add A
Little Spice To Your Meals

Condiments

Spiced Crab Apples

8 pounds crab apples
8½ cups sugar
1 quart cider vinegar
2 cups water
7 3-inch sticks cinnamon
2 tablespoons whole cloves
2 tablespoons whole allspice
Red food coloring

Wash crab apples; do not remove stems, but scrape out blossom ends. Combine sugar, vinegar and water. Tie spices in cheesecloth bag; add. Cook, covered, 10 minutes. Tint bright red food coloring. Add crab apples; cover; boil 10 minutes, or until tender. Let crab apples stand in syrup overnight. Drain; remove spice bag. Pack crab apples at once in clean hot jars. Bring syrup to boil; pour at once over crab apples. Adjust covers as manufacturer directs. Set jars on wire rack in deep kettle, with enough boiling water to cover tops of jars 1 inch. Cover kettle. Process (boil) 30 minutes, counting time after active boiling begins. Remove jars, adjust seals at once as manufacturer directs. Makes 4 to 5 quarts.

Spiced Apple Pie Filling For Canning

5 cups sliced apples (about 7 medium-size apples)
Large bowl salted water (1 tablespoon salt for each quart of water)
½ to ¾ cup sugar (depending on sweetness desired)
¼ teaspoon cinnamon
⅛ teaspoon nutmeg
1 tablespoon tapioca
¼ to ½ cup water (depending on juiciness of apples)
1 tablespoon lemon juice

Wash, core, peel, slice and measure apples into salt water. (Do not leave in salt water longer than 20 minutes; rinse before cooking.) Mix sugar, spices, tapioca and water. Stir over low heat until sugar is dissolved. Add apples; bring to boil over moderate heat; lower heat; cover and simmer 10 to 15 minutes, or until slices are barely tender. Add lemon juice. If juice is thick, add a little boiling water to thin to consistency of honey. Pack hot apple mixture to within ½-inch of the top of 1½ pint fruit jar. Run knife down between apples and side of jar to remove air bubbles. Adjust lid according to manufacturer's directions. Process 20 minutes in boiling water bath. Remove jars; complete seal, if necessary. Cool upright, away from drafts. Label. Each jar makes enough filling for 8-inch pie.

Apple Butter

5 pounds tart apples
2 cups apple cider
Sugar
¾ teaspoon ground cloves
½ teaspoon allspice
3 teaspoons cinnamon
½ teaspoon nutmeg

Wash, remove stems and quarter apples. Add cider; cook slowly until apples are soft. Put apples through food mill or sieve. Measure. Add ½ to ⅔ cup sugar for each cup of pulp, depending on the tartness of the apples. Add spices; mix well. Cook over low heat, stirring constantly, until sugar dissolves. Continue to cook, stirring often, until mixture sheets from spoon. Ladle into hot sterilized jars. Seal at once. Makes about 3 pints.

Apple Chutney

2 pounds apples
2 medium onions
2 pounds ripe tomatoes
1 pound seedless raisins
1 pound brown sugar
1 quart vinegar
¼ teaspoon cayenne
1 tablespoon ground ginger
1 teaspoon ground allspice
1 teaspoons ground nutmeg
¼ teaspoon ground cloves
2 teaspoons salt

Peel and chop apples, onions and tomatoes. Add remaining ingredients. Bring mixture to boiling, lower heat and simmer 1 hour, or until thick. Ladle into clean hot half-pint jars. Seal and label. Makes about 4 half pints.

Apple Relish

1 pint cider vinegar
3 cups honey
1 teaspoon ground cloves
1 teaspoon ground cinnamon
5 pounds cooking apples, peeled, cored and quartered

Heat together the vinegar, honey, cloves and cinnamon; then add the apples. Boil for 45 minutes, stirring frequently. Pour into sterilized jars; seal at once. Serve with cold meat of any kind.

Apple Jelly

Measure apple juice.   Add 1 cup of sugar to each cup. Stir until sugar dissolves. Boil rapidly until a good jelly test results. Skim; pour into glasses at once. Paraffin. Cool. Put on covers and labels.

Condiments

Apple Cardamom Jelly

Cut 4 pounds tart cooking apples into quarters; do not pare or core. Add 2 quarts water and 2 tablespoons cardamom seeds (removed from pods). Cook until apples are soft—about 25 minutes. Strain through dampened jelly bag. Makes about 7½ cups juice. Measure juice; tint a delicate pink with pure food coloring; add 1 cup sugar to each cup juice. Stir over low heat until sugar dissolves. Boil rapidly to 221°–223° on a candy-jelly thermometer, or until a good jelly test results. Skim. Pour into hot sterilized jelly glasses at once. Paraffin at once. Let cool. Put on covers and label. Makes about eight 8-ounce glasses of jelly.

Apple Herb Jelly

Wash 4 pounds ripe apples; do not peel or core. Cut in eighths. Add 6½ cups water; bring to boil; simmer, covered, 10 minutes, or until apples are soft. Crush with masher; simmer, covered, 5 minutes longer. Strain through cheesecloth. There should be about 5 cups. Measure 2½ cups of juice into saucepan. Bring to a boil and pour over ¼ cup dried herb.*

Let stand 15 minutes; strain through cheesecloth into large enamel or agate saucepan. Add ¼ cup vinegar and 4 cups sugar; mix well. Place over high heat; bring to a boil. (While mixture is coming to a boil, add a few drops red or green food coloring, if desired.) Add ½ bottle fruit pectin. Bring to a *full rolling boil;* boil hard 1 minute, stirring constantly. Remove from heat; skim off foam; pour quickly into jelly glasses. Cover jelly at once with ⅛-inch hot melted paraffin. Makes about 6 medium glasses. Repeat, using remaining juice and a different herb.

Apple Mint Jelly

Measure apple juice. Add a large bunch of fresh mint. Boil 15 minutes, skimming frequently. Remove mint. Add ¾ cup sugar to each cup of juice. Stir until sugar dissolves. Add enough food coloring to tint deep mint green. Boil rapidly until a good jelly test results. Skim. Pour into glasses at once. Paraffin. Cool. Put on covers, and label.

Sage, tarragon, thyme, marjoram, savory or mint.

Apple Pear Conserve

2 cups chopped, unpared cooking apples	½ cup lemon juice
	3 cups sugar
2 cups chopped fresh pears (or peaches)	1 cup chopped walnuts

Combine all ingredients except nuts; cook slowly until apple is transparent—about 20 minutes. Add walnuts. Pour into hot sterilized glasses. Seal immediately. Makes seven 6-ounce glasses.

Spicy Apple Relish

4 pounds onions	1 teaspoon powdered cloves
3 pounds green apples	1 tablespoon cinnamon
4½ cups brown sugar, firmly packed	1 teaspoon allspice
	1 tablespoon salt
1 pound raisins	¼ cup molasses
2 teaspoons ginger	

Put onions and apples through food chopper, using coarse knife. Combine all ingredients in large kettle; simmer, uncovered, about 2 hours, or until mixture is thick and dark. Stir occasionally to prevent sticking. Pour into hot sterilized half-pint jars. Seal at once. Makes about 3 quarts.

Puchidee Relish

6 large, tart apples	¼ cup dairy sour cream
1 medium onion	
½ green pepper	½ teaspoon salt
½ sweet red pepper	Few grains pepper

Pare, core and dice apples. Mince onion and peppers; add to apples. Add sour cream, salt and pepper; mix well. Chill 1 hour. Makes 8 servings.

Raw Apple Relish

2 large red apples	1 tablespoon capers
Juice of 1 lemon	¼ cup sliced ripe olives
1 medium onion, chopped	
	½ cup French dressing
¼ cup sliced sweet gherkins	

Core apples; do not peel. Cut crosswise into ½-inch slices, then into ½-inch chunks. Sprinkle with lemon juice. Add remaining ingredients; toss to mix well. Makes 6 servings.

Chart For Comparing Varieties

APPLE BUYING GUIDE

(An abbreviated guide for buying and using apple varieties. Supplies are, of course, more limited toward the end of the indicated period of availability and available longer for those varieties stored in controlled atmosphere storage, which extends the market season by several months. Some varieties are more universally distributed than others. In the final analysis use is a matter of preference. All varieties can be eaten fresh for snacks, for salads, etc., all can be baked and cooked. Our suggested uses are based on the characteristics of each variety and our experiences with each variety in our Apple Kitchen.)

VARIETY	WHEN AVAILABLE	WHERE AVAILABLE IN U.S. & CANADA				VARIETY CHARACTERISTICS	RANGE OF USES	BEST USES	SPECIAL NOTES
		EAST	CTRL.	SOUTH	WEST				
SUMMER & EARLY FALL VARIETIES	July–September	x	x	x	x	Numerous varieties, Red, Green and Yellow. Tender, tart and juicy	Snacks, salads, fruit cups and all culinary uses	Sauce and all culinary uses except whole baked apples	Numerous summer and early fall varieties are available, distribution limited from area to area—none is universally distributed. (Lodi, Puritan, Summer Rambo, Williams Red, Crimson Beauty, Early McIntosh, Julyred, Starr, Melba, Tydeman's Red, Summer Champion and many others)
WEALTHY	Aug.–October	x	x			Two-toned Red and Green, usually striped or blushed with red. Tart and spicy	Snacks, salads, fruit cups and all culinary uses	Sauce and all culinary uses except whole baked apples	Declining production; limited fresh availability and distribution—mostly New York, Ontario, Michigan, Wisconsin. Major supply is commercially processed
GRAVEN-STEIN	Aug.–October	x			x	Red striped or blushed, Tart, spicy and juicy	Snacks, salads, fruit cups and all culinary uses	Sauce and all culinary uses except whole baked apples	Limited fresh distribution except in California. Limited availability in northeastern U.S. and Canada. Major production is commercially processed
RED DELICIOUS	Sept.–June	x	x	x	x	Bright Red. Sweet and Juicy	Snacks, salads and fruit cups	Snacks, salads and fruit cups	Most universally grown and available of all apple varieties
GOLDEN DELICIOUS	Sept.–June	x	x	x	x	Yellow-Green to Bright Yellow, often light burnished or russeted when grown in East. Sweet and juicy	Snacks, salads, fruit cups, baking and all culinary uses	Snacks, salads, fruit cups, baking, sauce and all culinary uses	Most universally available all-purpose variety
McINTOSH	Sept.–June	x	x	x	x	Two-toned Red and Green, Slightly tart, tender, juicy, spritely, aromatic	Snacks, salads, fruit cups, sauce, all culinary uses	Snacks, salads, fruit cups, sauce and all culinary uses except baked whole apples	Less generally available in South-western and Central-western U.S.
JONATHAN	Sept.–April	x	x	x	x	Bright Red. Slightly tart, rich flavored and juicy	Snacks, salads, fruit cups and all culinary uses	Snacks, salads, fruit cups, sauce and all culinary uses	Less generally available in Northeast and Southwest during early and late months of the season. Well distributed during much of season except in Northeast
CORTLAND	Sept.–May	x	x			Red and Green two-toned color with purplish undertone on red. Snow-white flesh, mildly tart, juicy and tender	Snacks, salads, fruit cups, all culinary uses	Snacks, salads, fruit cups, baking, sauce and all culinary uses	Distribution and availability, mostly in northeastern U.S. and Canada and in Midwest. Excellent snack, salad and fruit cup apple and excellent but tender baking and cooking variety

Chart For Comparing Varieties

APPLE BUYING GUIDE (cont.)

VARIETY	WHEN AVAILABLE	WHERE AVAILABLE IN U.S. & CANADA				VARIETY CHARACTERISTICS	RANGE OF USES	BEST USES	SPECIAL NOTES
		EAST	CTRL.	SOUTH	WEST				
STAYMAN	Oct.–May	x	x	x		Deep Red with purplish undertone, often slightly burnished or russeted. Rich flavored, moderately juicy	Snacks, salads, fruit cups, and all culinary uses	Snacks, salads, fruit cups, sauce and all culinary uses	Distribution and availability, mostly in Middle Atlantic and southeastern U.S.—Pennsylvania to Florida
ROME BEAUTY	Oct.–June	x	x	x	x	Bright Red, sometimes striped. Very mildly tart	Snacks, salads, fruit cups, baking and all culinary uses	Baking and all culinary uses	Produced and available in all areas of U.S. Less available in Canada. A fair fresh eating apple, but best for baked and cooked uses
YORK IMPERIAL	Oct.–June	x		x		Green with varying degrees of Red. Lopsided in shape, mildly tart	All culinary uses, snacks, salads and fruit cups	Baking, sauce, all culinary uses	Limited fresh distribution and availability—mostly in Appalachian area and Southeast. Major supply is utilized for commercial processing
RHODE ISLAND GREENING	Oct.–April	x	x			Green to Yellow-Green. Mildly tart	All culinary uses	Baking, sauce and all culinary uses	Limited fresh distribution and availability, mostly in New York, New England, Michigan and other upper central states. Major supply is utilized for commercial processing. Variety sometimes confused with Northwest Greening, which is an earlier maturing variety, more generally available, particularly August–December
NEWTOWN PIPPIN	Oct.–May				x	Green to Yellow-Green. Mildly tart. Less juicy than some other varieties	Snacks, salads, baking and all culinary uses	Baking, sauce and all culinary uses	Very limited local supply seasonally in Virginia; major fresh distribution and availability in California, Oregon, Washington. Large part of supply utilized for commercial processing
SPARTAN	Oct.–April	x	x		x	Bright Red. Mildly tart, crisp and juicy	Snacks, salads, fruit cups, culinary uses	Snacks, salads, fruit cups	One of newer varieties (McIntosh x Yellow Newtown, 1935), excellent dessert quality. Limited distribution and availability, mostly British Columbia and West Coast, but some in Northeast
WINESAP	Nov.–July	x	x	x	x	Deep Red. Moderately tart, rich wine-like flavor, juicy	Snacks, salads, fruit cups and all culinary uses	Snacks, salads, fruit cups, sauce and all culinary uses	A late season apple available in most markets from December through June, but declining in production and distribution
GRANNY SMITH	Oct.–July	x	x	x	x	Bright Green, very firm, quite tart	Snacks, salads, fruit cups and all culinary uses	Snacks, salads, all cooking	While relatively new in the U.S., Granny Smith has long been in demand elsewhere around the world

APPLE BUYING GUIDE (cont.)

VARIETY	WHEN AVAILABLE	WHERE AVAILABLE IN U.S. & CANADA				VARIETY CHARACTERISTICS	RANGE OF USES	BEST USES	SPECIAL NOTES
		EAST	WEST	SOUTH	CTRL.				
EMPIRE	Sept.–May	x	x			Mostly carmine red; slightly tart; good keeper	Snacks, salad and fruit cups	Snacks	One of the newer varieties, Empire is the product of a cross between Red Delicious and McIntosh, and captures the flavor qualities of both
MUTSU	Oct.–May	x	x			Green-Gold in color; mildly tart; similar to Golden Delicious, one of its parents, except that is a little more tart	Snacks, salads and all culinary uses	All culinary uses	This Golden Delicious type apple, a Japanese development is the product of a cross between Golden Delicious and a Japanese variety, In-do
NORTHERN SPY	Nov.–May	x	x			Two-toned Red and Green. Moderately tart, rich flavored, crisp and juicy	Snacks, salads, fruit cups, baking and all culinary uses	Snacks, salads, fruit cups, baking and all culinary uses	Like Golden Delicious, Northern Spy is one of the finest all-purpose varieties grown. Unfortunately it is declining in supply. Limited fresh distribution and availability, mostly in New York, Michigan and Ontario, Canada. Major supply is utilized for commercial processing
IDARED	Sept.–May	x	x			Bright Red, sometimes with Green shoulder; moderately tart, very juicy and spritely flavor	Snacks, fruit cups and salads; excellent for applesauce and most culinary uses	Snacks, salads and fruit cups and applesauce	One of very popular newer varieties available mostly in the Great Lakes area and northeast part of the U.S.

*Specific areas indicated are major areas of production and availability. Increasingly, however, all major apple varieties are available throughout the U.S. and Canada, and increasingly the year around.

A number of other excellent old varieties—and a number of fine new varieties—are available in all producing areas. Distribution is generally limited to the area of production, hence we have not charted them. They include:

Twenty Ounce, excellent culinary apple, seasonally available (September–January) in western New York. *N.W. Greening*, late summer and early fall culinary apple, seasonally available in Appalachian and Great Lakes areas; *Haralson* and *Connell Red*, good all-purpose varieties generally available (October–February), Minnesota and Wisconsin. *Macoun*, excellent dessert quality, McIntosh type, highest flavor rating; limited availability in Northeast and North Central areas; *Idared*, a relatively new late-season Jonathan-type variety, good all purpose, available in Northeast and North Central areas. These and a number of other old and new varieties seasonally available in areas of production.

Tools

Patent Pending

CORRUGATED APPLE WEDGER

To cut fancy apple wedges and core the apple in one stroke, center apple stem in middle ring of the Corrugated Apple Wedger.

Use side grippers and hold wedger in a horizontal position to the top of the apple.

Use a firm downward pressure passing the device completely through the apple.

THUMB DECORATOR/PEELER

1. Slide on Thumb Decorator/Peeler as shown sloping at 180° when you want to decorate.

2. Slide on Thumb Decorator/Peeler in position as shown at 90° when you want to peel.

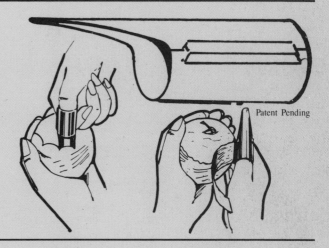

Patent Pending

APPLE CORER

1. Before using, make sure the disappearing blade is in the up position.

2. Place the corer over the center of the apple, press down and rotate it back and forth until you reach the desired depth.

3. Without removing corer from the apple, slide the disappearing blade all the way down with your thumb.

Make several complete turns and lift out.

PARING KNIFE

This sharp, flexible paring knife is ideal for peeling and decorating.

If you cannot find these tools at your local culinary store, contact the publisher.

Some Favorite Varieties And Uses

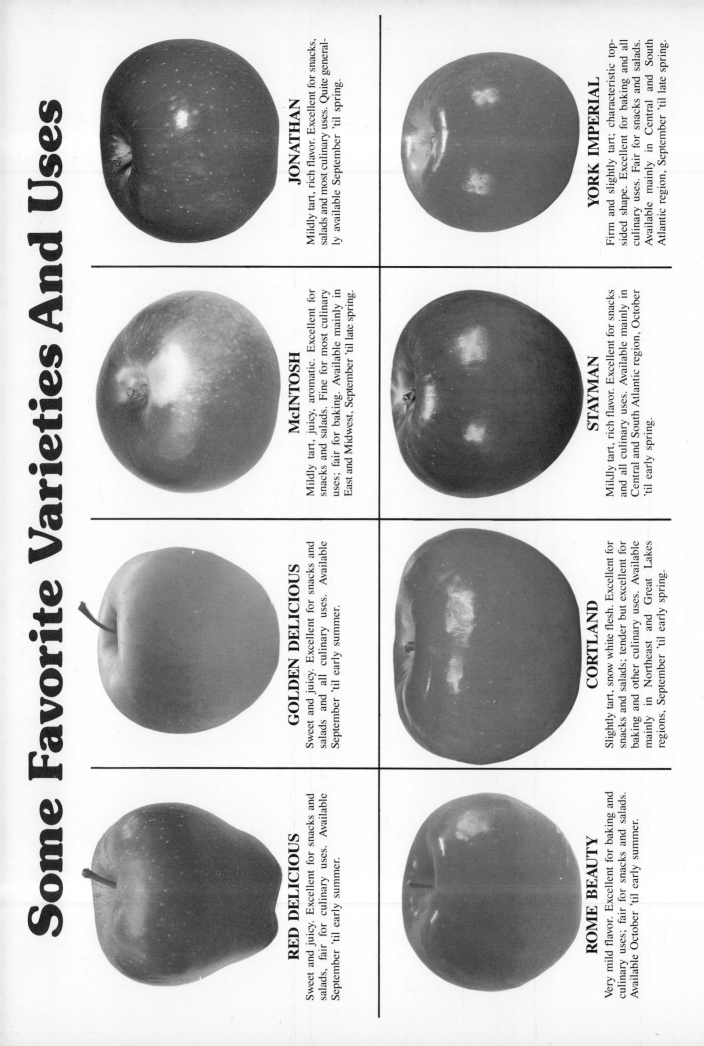

JONATHAN

Mildly tart, rich flavor. Excellent for snacks, salads and most culinary uses. Quite generally available September 'til spring.

McINTOSH

Mildly tart, juicy, aromatic. Excellent for snacks and salads. Fine for most culinary uses; fair for baking. Available mainly in East and Midwest, September 'til late spring.

GOLDEN DELICIOUS

Sweet and juicy. Excellent for snacks and salads and all culinary uses. Available September 'til early summer.

RED DELICIOUS

Sweet and juicy. Excellent for snacks and salads, fair for culinary uses. Available September 'til early summer.

YORK IMPERIAL

Firm and slightly tart; characteristic top-sided shape. Excellent for baking and all culinary uses. Fair for snacks and salads. Available mainly in Central and South Atlantic region, September 'til late spring.

STAYMAN

Mildly tart, rich flavor. Excellent for snacks and all culinary uses. Available mainly in Central and South Atlantic region, October 'til early spring.

CORTLAND

Slightly tart, snow white flesh. Excellent for snacks and salads; tender but excellent for baking and other culinary uses. Available mainly in Northeast and Great Lakes regions, September 'til early spring.

ROME BEAUTY

Very mild flavor. Excellent for baking and culinary uses; fair for snacks and salads. Available October 'til early summer.

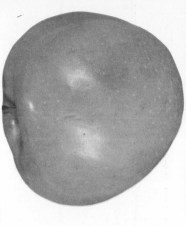

RHODE ISLAND GREENING

Mildly tart; excellent cooking and baking variety. Utilized primarily for commercial processing for frozen and canned sliced apples. Available in fresh form mostly in northeast during fall months.

GRAVENSTEIN

Tart, juicy. Excellent for all culinary and salad uses, except fair for baking. Fine for snacks. Available mainly on West coast, August 'til early fall.

EMPIRE

Mildly tart, juicy, aromatic. A cross between Red Delicious and McIntosh, with the excellent flavor qualities of both. Excellent for snacks and salads. Fine for most culinary uses. Available mainly in east and upper midwest, late September 'til late spring.

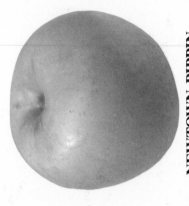

NEWTOWN PIPPIN

Mildly tart, firm. Excellent for all baking and culinary uses; fine for snacks and salads. Available mainly on West coast September 'til spring.

NORTHERN SPY

Moderately tart, rich flavor. Excellent for snacks, salads, baking and all culinary uses. Limitedly available mainly in Northeast and Great Lakes regions.

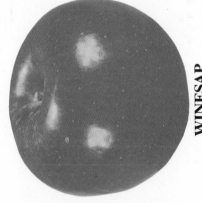

WINESAP

Moderately tart, firm. Excellent for snacks, salads and all culinary uses. Mostly late season availability. November 'til early summer; declining in volume.

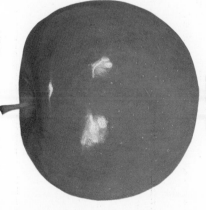

IDARED

Moderately tart and juicy, with Jonathan like flavor. An excellent all purpose variety. Available mostly in east and midwest. This variety is a cross between Jonathan and Wagener. Fruit size averages medium to large.

GRANNY SMITH

A moderately tart, very firm, spritely flavored variety. Popular for snacks, salads and all culinary uses. Generally available year around from U.S. or imported sources.

To Keep Them Best, Keep Them Refrigerated.

For the best results, choose a fresh apple that is well rounded, without blemishes or bruises.
A sharp serrated steak knife is recommended for cutting.
Cut off ⅓ from the side of the apple to provide a stable base.
This section will be used later to make the head and neck.

Place the apple cut side down with the stem facing you.
Use a light sawing motion to make a small wedge shaped cut at the top.
Continue making wedge shaped cuts each a bit larger than the previous one.
The size of the apple and the thickness of the wedge will determine how many wedges you can make.
Repeat this procedure on both sides, forming three sets of feathers.

If a piece breaks, don't worry, the sections will fit together and the break will not be noticeable.

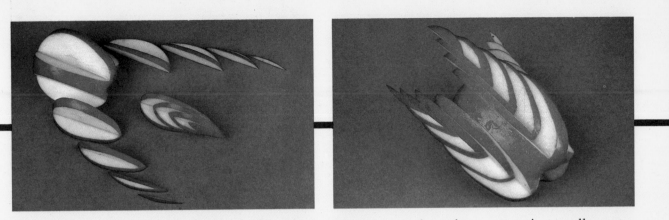

To create the wings and tail feathers start with the largest cut and overlap consecutive smaller cuts.
Piece the wedges together evenly giving a fanned out appearance.
The natural juices of the apple hold the feathers together.
Throughout the book various head and neck shapes are shown.
Choose your favorite to complete the apple bird.

Cut a ¼ inch slice from the center of the section set aside in the first step.
Carve this section as shown in the photograph.

Another variation can be made by cutting a "v" at the front, leaving some flesh for the head and then following the contour of the peel. Cloves or appleseeds may be used to make eyes.

Attach the head and neck with a toothpick.
Prevent darkening by squeezing lemon juice over the entire surface of the apple bird.
To present the apple bird, use a potato for a base, cover it with greens and insert two toothpicks into the top.
Attach the bird in a dive bomb position and display.

(See Photo Next Page)

Stuffed Apple
Cheese
Platter

Garnish

An attractive and easy-to-make cheese platter can be made using tools described on Page 33.

Core a large, fresh apple using the apple corer.

Stuff the cored apple with cream cheese and chill until firm.

After chilling, cut the apple into slices as shown, top with strawberries or your favorite fruit.

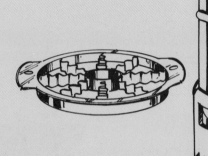

Enhance your cheese platter with fancy apple wedges.

The corrugated apple wedger cores and cuts decorative apple wedges in one stroke.

Arrange the wedges in an attractive manner on your platter using various cheese varieties.

Apple Eagle

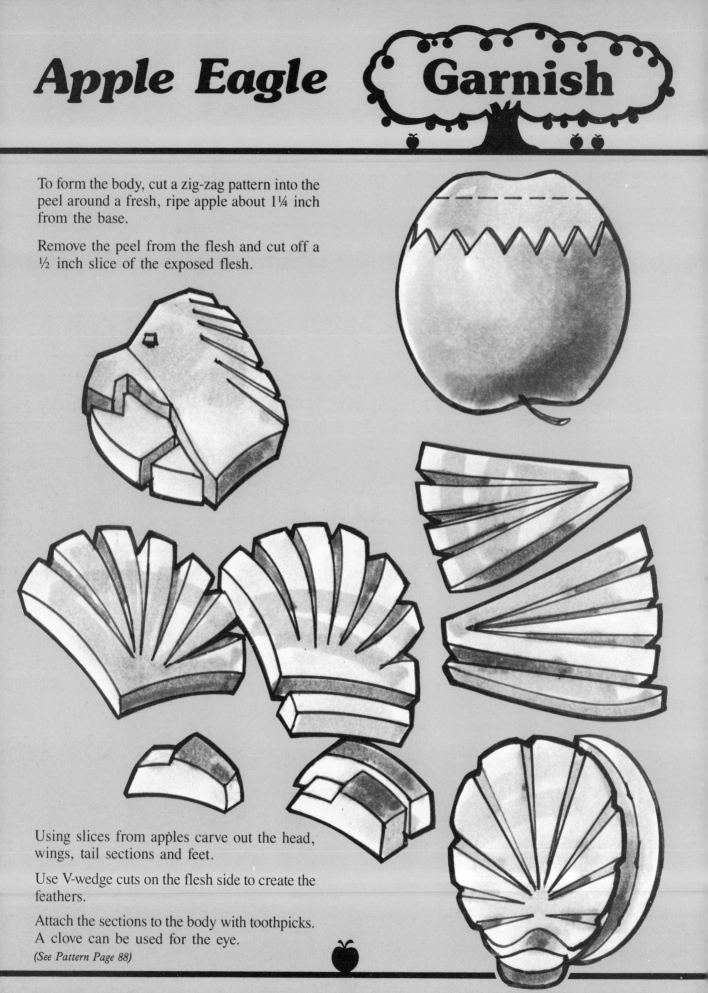

To form the body, cut a zig-zag pattern into the peel around a fresh, ripe apple about 1¼ inch from the base.

Remove the peel from the flesh and cut off a ½ inch slice of the exposed flesh.

Using slices from apples carve out the head, wings, tail sections and feet.

Use V-wedge cuts on the flesh side to create the feathers.

Attach the sections to the body with toothpicks. A clove can be used for the eye.

(See Pattern Page 88)

48

Apple Baskets

There are many designs for the apple basket. You are limited only by your imagination. Select a large apple and cut a slice from the bottom to form a stable base.

Cut away two wedges at the top of the apple. Remove the flesh from the inside so that you are left with a basket and a handle in the middle. Be careful to leave a ¼″ of flesh on the apple for strength.

Fill the basket with desired fruit, cranberry or apple sauce.
Attach a strawberry to the handle with a toothpick.

50

Apple Coaches

Since these garnishes are slightly more intricate, outline guides have been provided to form the various parts.

Use a ¾" slice from the side of an apple cut flat on each side to provide a stable base for the coach.

Select the coach you wish to make and using the outline guide provided carve out the body of the coach.

To form the wheels, fenders and lights use the guides provided to carve the parts from apple slices.

Decorate the parts and add details as shown.

The seat of the coach is carved from slices of apples decorated with V-wedge cuts.

Carve the windows from sections of apples as shown.

Form the top of the coach with slices of apples decorated with V-wedge cuts topped with a cherry or strawberry.

(See Pattern Page 87)

52

Twin Birds  Garnish

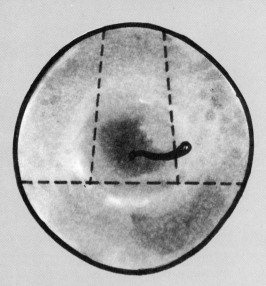

Cut a slice from the side of a large apple, just below the stem.

You can use either the flesh or peel side of this slice to carve the head and neck.

From the remaining piece of apple cut a ¾ " section from the middle.

This piece will be used for the body.

Carve the wings from the remaining side pieces.

Use V-wedge cuts on the flesh side to form the feathers.

Using three slices from the sides of another apple carve the tail sections.

Feathers are created with V-wedge cuts on the flesh side.

Attach the head, wings and tail sections to the body with toothpicks.

Use a clove for the eye.

Bird of Paradise

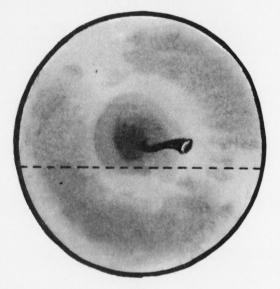

This garnish can be made from one apple.

Cut a slice from the side of an apple just below the stem.

Cut the slice you have just made into thirds.

The top slice will be used for the base, the middle slice for the tail and the bottom slice, with the most peel, will be used for the head and neck.

Using the peel side, from the bottom slice, create the head and neck as shown.

Carve out the beak and eye from the peel.

From the middle slice of apple, carve out the tail piece.

Use V-wedge cuts as shown to form the feathers.

To form the body cut a ¾" slice from the center of the remaining piece of apple and mount it on the base with toothpicks.

The wings are formed by cutting the two remaining side pieces into as many equal slices as possible.

The larger the apple, the more wing slices can be made.

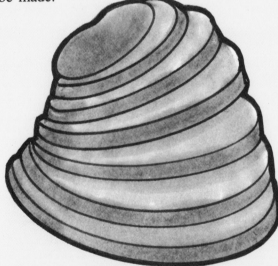

To form the wings, overlap each slice as shown, exposing part of the flesh of each slice until all slices are used.

Repeat the process for the other wing.

Carve the crown from another piece of apple using V-wedge cuts on the flesh side as shown.

Attach the head, crown and tail to the body with toothpicks.

Position the wings next to the body and secure with toothpicks.

(See front cover photograph as reference.)

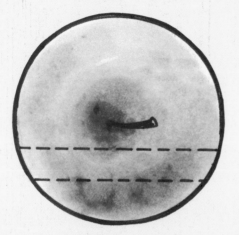

Cut a ¾ " slice from the side of a large fresh apple.

This section will be used to carve out the head and neck.

Cut a ⅜" slice from the same side of the apple, just below the stem, to be used as the base.

There are several variations of the head and neck you can make by using either the flesh or peel side of the apple.

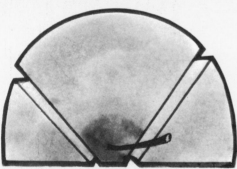

Cut a wedge-shaped section from the remaining piece of apple.

This will be used for the body.

Slice the wedge-shaped section into four V-wedges as shown in the photo.

Slide each of the four V-wedges back slightly to form the feathered body.

Attach the body and head to the base with a toothpick.

Use a clove for the eye.

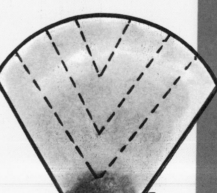

Design Cutters

Use a vegetable or cookie cutter to cut out various designs from an apple.

Twelve different cutting designs are available from ICC including the lobster, butterfly, rabbit, tulip, goat, fish, maple leaf, crab, dove, hen, dragon and rooster.

Select the design you wish to make.

Hold the cutter at right angles to the side of the apple and push in to form the design.

Cut a slice from the side of the apple where you have formed the design.

Carefully remove the design from the slice as shown.

Display the design on the flesh side of an apple section with the peel side showing.

For an inlaid effect cut the same design into the flesh side of an apple section and remove the design.

Insert the design with peel attached into the opening.

It will fit perfectly because it was made from the same cutter.

For variation, the procedure can be reversed by inserting a design cut from the flesh of an apple into a section of apple where the peel is the background.

To preserve and add a shiny appearance coat the completed garnish with clear gelatin.

If your local culinary store does not carry the desired cutters, contact ICC.

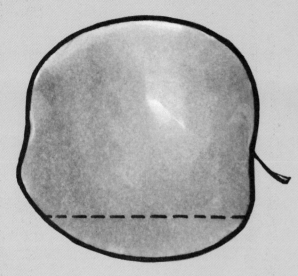

This garnish is made from more than one apple. Cut a slice from the side of an apple to be used for the body.

Carve out the body from the flesh side of the apple slice as shown.

The wings are formed from other slices carved from the flesh side.

Use V-wedge cuts to form the feathers as shown.

Attach the wings to the body with toothpicks and use a clove for the eye.

To form the base, cut a slice from the side of a large apple exposing the flesh.
Using the peel side from the apple slice, carve out a small dove and attach it to the exposed flesh of the apple as shown.
Attach the doves to the apple base with wooden skewers and decorate with baby's breath.

Lovebird

Garnish

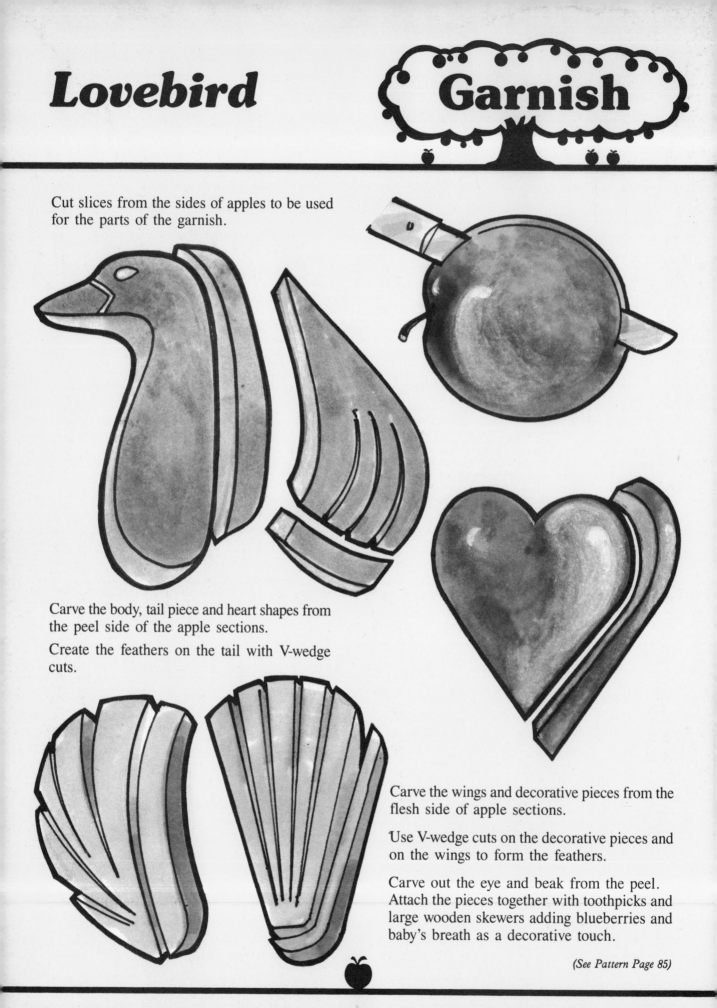

Cut slices from the sides of apples to be used for the parts of the garnish.

Carve the body, tail piece and heart shapes from the peel side of the apple sections.

Create the feathers on the tail with V-wedge cuts.

Carve the wings and decorative pieces from the flesh side of apple sections.

Use V-wedge cuts on the decorative pieces and on the wings to form the feathers.

Carve out the eye and beak from the peel. Attach the pieces together with toothpicks and large wooden skewers adding blueberries and baby's breath as a decorative touch.

(See Pattern Page 85)

Neptune's Pride

Cut slices from the sides of apples for the sections to be carved into the parts of the fish.

Carve the sections as shown on the peel side of the apple slice.

Use V-wedge cuts to form the detail.
Attach the sections together with toothpicks.

(See Pattern Page 84)

66

Use a sharp knife to cut the shape of petals around a large, fresh apple.

Cut into the peel and remove the unwanted skin.

Carefully peel back the petals leaving them attached to the apple.

Remove ¾ of the peeled section as shown.

The remaining piece of apple will form the center of the flower and the petals.

Make V-wedge cuts from the center to the outer edge of the flesh to create a decorative pattern.

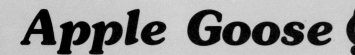

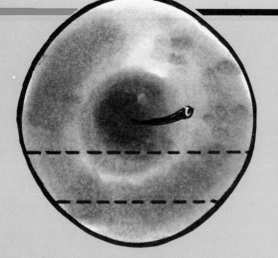

Cut a ⅜″ slice from the side of a large apple to be used to form the head and neck.

Cut another slice just below the stem which will be used for the base.

Carve the head and neck from the peel-side and cut away part of the peel to form the beak and eye.

From the remaining piece of apple cut a ¾″ section from the middle.

This piece will be used for the body.

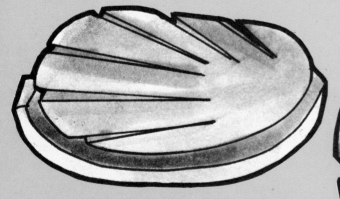

Carve the wings from the remaining side pieces using V-wedge cuts on the flesh side to form the feathers.

Cut three slices from the sides of another apple to make the tail sections.

Use V-wedge cuts on the flesh side to form feathers.

Attach the head, wings and tail sections to the body with toothpicks; then place the goose on the base.

Mr. Peacock

Garnish

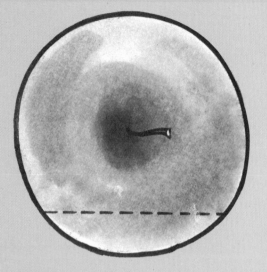

Obviously, this garnish is made from several apples.

Cut a ¾ " slice from the side of a large apple to form a stable base for the body.

Use the slice from the side to carve the head and neck from the flesh of the apple as shown.

Cut slices from the sides of other apples to form the wings and tail sections.

The wings and tail pieces are the same basic shape.

Use V-wedge cuts on the flesh side of the slice to create the feathers.

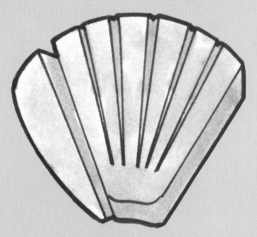

Carve the crown of the peacock from a section of apple and decorate with V-wedge cuts as shown.

Attach the crown, head, wings and tail sections in position with toothpicks.

Decorate the tail sections with kiwi and strawberry slices topped with blueberries.

Hold them in position with a toothpick. Use a seed or clove for the eye.

Ms. Peacock

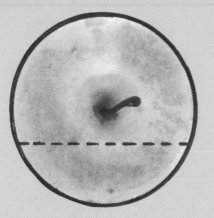

This garnish is made from more than one apple.

Cut a slice from the side of a large apple, just below the stem, to form a stable base for the body.

The slice from the side is used to make the tail piece as shown.

Use V-wedge cuts on the flesh side of the slice to create the feathers.

Cut slices from sides of other apples to form the wings.

Use V-wedge cuts on the flesh side of the slice to create the feathers.

Carve the head and neck from a flesh section of apple as shown.

___

Using toothpicks, attach the crown, head, wings and tail piece in position as shown.

To finish off the tail, alternate large wooden skewers of blueberries with skewers of sliced kiwis topped with the carved apple tear-drops.

Insert the skewers into the tail piece and use a seed or a clove for the eye.

Create the crown for the head and the tear-drop shapes for the tail by carving from the peel-side of apple pieces.

Apple Shells  Garnish

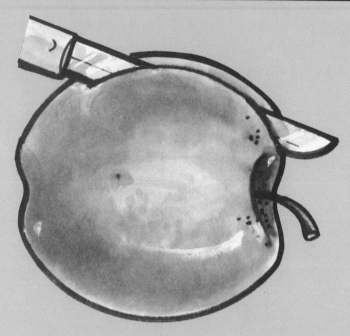

Cut 1 inch slices from the sides of a fresh, ripe apple.

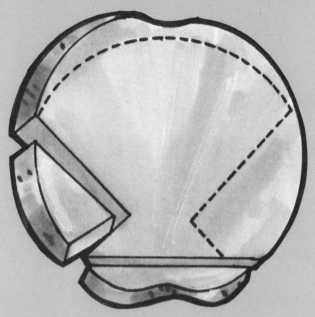

Cut each slice to the shape of the shell.

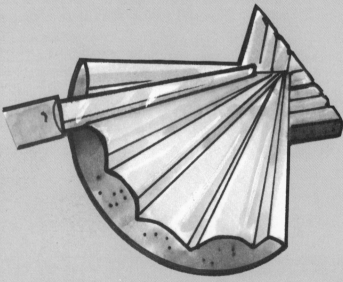

Use a sharp knife to carve V-wedge cuts on the flesh side of the shell.

To make V-wedge cuts, cut on an angle from the center to the outer edge and then complete the V-cut from the opposite angle.

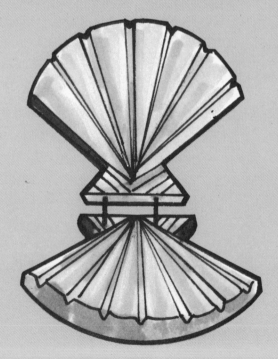

Attach two shells together with toothpicks. Decorate the shells with assorted fruit.

Apple Swan

Cut a ½ inch slice from the side of an apple to provide a stable base.

Use the slice from the base section to create the tail.

Decorate the tail piece with V-wedge cuts on the flesh side.

Cut a ⅜ inch slice from each side of the apple to form the wings.

Cut each slice into wing shapes.

Use V-wedge cuts on the flesh side to form the feathers.

Carve the head and neck from a section of apple as shown.

Cut out the eye and beak from the peel.

Attach the tail, wings and head to the body with toothpicks.

(See Pattern Page 89)

78

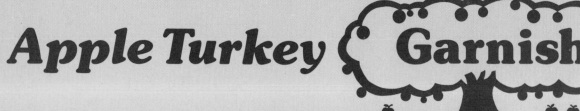

Cut a slice from the side of a large apple to form a stable base for the body.

Cut the slice you have just made in half lengthwise and join the two halves together flesh side to flesh side.
Carve out the head and neck as shown and use cloves for eyes.

To complete the body and form the wings cut a slice from the bottom of the apple.

The wings are formed by cutting V-wedges into the side of the apple.
The first V-wedge will be small and each succeeding V-wedge will be a little larger than the previous one.
Slide the V-shaped sections up fanning them to form the wings.
Repeat the process for the other wing.

To form the tail sections cut slices from the sides of another apple, decorate with V-wedge cuts then attach to the body with toothpicks.

Attach the head and neck to the body with toothpicks. An alternate head and neck is shown carved from the flesh side of an apple section. (Opposite Page.)

Cut a bright, green Granny Smith apple in half as shown and remove the stem.

Decorate half of the apple with cross-cuts into the peel side to form the turtle shell.

Cut the remaining half into four equal slices.

Carve the head and tail from two of the slices.

Cut the four legs from the remaining two slices as shown.

Attach the head to the stem end of the apple with a toothpick.

Use cloves for eyes.

Attach the legs and tail with toothpicks.

Fish

Pattern

(See Photo Page 67)

Love Bird Pattern

(See Photo Page 65)

Pattern

(See Photo Page 53)

Coach

Pattern

(See Photo Page 53)

87

Eagle

(See Photo Page 49)

Swan

(See Photo Page 79)

89

The following are examples of wings, necks, tails and crowns. I have selected some of my favorite variations that can be used to elaborate upon the garnishes shown. Of course these are not the only designs that may be used. An adept garnisher can create changes to give a garnish an original look.

The photographs show the flesh side of the apple. Create a brand new garnish by using the peel side of the apple rather than the flesh side. Use different colored apples to create multi-colored birds. This enables you to create a myriad of colorful combinations by making different parts of the bird out of different colored apples.

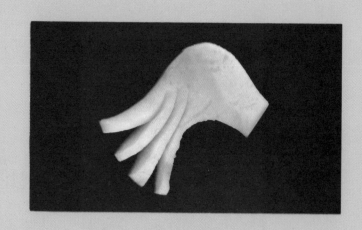

Variations

Complete Your Library

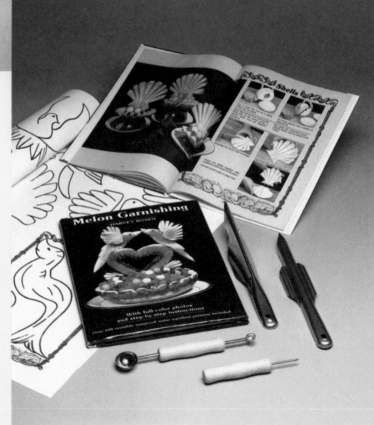

HOW TO GARNISH By Harvey Rosen

How To Garnish is more than just the most useful and informative book about food garnishing. It's also the easiest to learn from, because it combines easy-to-follow instructions with illustrations that show exactly what to do. No guesswork involved; everything you need to know is right here. This washable hardcover book contains more than twenty full-color photographs and two hundred illustrations depicting a variety of arrangements that are easy to make. Complete with 5 Garnishing Tools: Corrugated Garnishing Blade, Spiral Slicer, Paring Knife and Food Decorator.

MELON GARNISHING By Harvey Rosen

Opening the book, Melon Garnishing, opens the door to an array of eye-appealing, taste-tempting, guest-amazing culinary creations that anyone can make using the techniques revealed in the book. Readers don't need any previous experience because the book makes everything simple. It provides easy-to-follow instructions and step-by-step drawings that make the actual preparation of the melons into a pleasurable, creative undertaking; the book turns work into fun.

Included with the book are over 100 full-size stencils to make the whole operation foolproof—just follow the lines to garnishing glory. (The stencils are all on one large sheet, so you don't have to worry about losing individual pieces.) The four beautifully designed tools accompanying the book are last-for-a-lifetime utensils. These helpful tools were designed to save time while giving melon garnishes a professional flair. The V-Decorator, U-Decorator, Melon Baller and the Sketching Tool are all crafted from heavy-gauge stainless steel and imported hardwoods, they make cutting and shaping operations a breeze.

HOW TO GARNISH (with tools) HT-1001 ISBN 0-96125-721-0
HOW TO GARNISH (book only) HT-1003 ISBN 0-96125-720-2
MELON GARNISHING (with patterns and tools) HT-1005 ISBN 0-9612572-4-5
MELON GARNISHING (with patterns, no tools) HT-1004 ISBN 0-9612572-3-7

INTERNATIONAL CULINARY CONSULTANTS
P.O. Box 2202 Elberon Station, Elberon, New Jersey 07740